COME HERE and COOK

JORDAN HOWLETT
with Noah Galuten

COME HERE and COOK

STORIES AND RECIPES FROM A LIFE AT THE TABLE

Photography by Max Milla

DK

DK | Penguin Random House

Publisher Mike Sanders
Executive Editor Alexander Rigby
Editorial Director Ann Barton
Art & Design Director William Thomas
Designer Joanna Price
Photographer Max Milla
Food Stylist Judean Sakimoto
Recipe Tester Bee Berrie
Editorial Assistant Resham Anand
Copy Editor Tiffany Taing
Proofreaders Bianca Bosman, Anna Wostenberg
Indexer Celia McCoy

First American Edition, 2026
Published in the United States by DK Publishing
1745 Broadway, 20th Floor, New York, NY 10019

The authorized representative in the EEA is Dorling Kindersley Verlag GmbH. Arnulfstr. 124, 80636 Munich, Germany

26 27 28 29 30 10 9 8 7 6 5 4 3 2 1
001-352291-NOV2026

Library of Congress Number: 2026935738
ISBN 979-8-2171-2981-2

Printed and bound in China

www.dk.com

MIX
Paper
FSC™ C018179

For my grandmother, Nikki—"Lela" to me—whose love of food, family, and bringing people together inspired this book from the very beginning.

Stories

Recipes

INTRODUCTION

When I was in college, all I wanted in the world was to become a professional baseball player. If you knew me back then, you knew I was single-minded in my focus. Life was baseball, and that was all that mattered. But there was something else almost nobody knew about me: I was battling with food insecurity. I was a young man burning so many calories, working out multiple times a day, all while hiding this terrifying feeling that I had no idea where my next few meals would come from.

Then one day I heard that if you hosted an event that benefits the students on campus, you can actually receive funding from the school. Since I knew a lot of students who were similarly food insecure, I thought this was my opportunity to host an event about mental health. But more than anything, I wanted to take those funds and make sure that, for at least a night, a group of people—myself included—could share a meal, take home leftovers, and feel safe and fed. I told everybody about it and started planning, and soon enough, the date was set and the guests were confirmed. Then all of a sudden, I found out our funding had been declined. At that point, I had already committed to the event, and I was not the kind of person capable of backing out. Already struggling to feed myself, I now had to find a way to feed dozens of others too.

I needed help. I reached out to my aunt, and any extended family members I could, to try to gather the funds to make the biggest, cheapest dinner I possibly could. We pulled together a humble sum of money and went shopping. I made spaghetti and tomato sauce, bought lots of cheap bread, loaded up on flour, sugar, and canned pineapples, and then made the ugliest bunch of pineapple upside-down cakes you've ever seen.

But it worked. The event came, there were lots of people, and there was plenty of food. I spoke first and told people about my dreams and my goals, opening up publicly in a way I never really had before. The other attendees, in response, got up and spoke too. It was beautiful. We talked about mental health, we shared food, and this event became a core, foundational memory in my life. It showed me the importance of food and the power it has to build community and connect people. As someone who struggled to find food for so long, it took this experience to learn that food is about so much more than just fuel: It's about people.

Food has become a very important part of my current job, too, one I'll admit is a very strange job. Some people would say I'm an "influencer." I wouldn't put it that way, even though between TikTok, YouTube, and Instagram I have, as of this writing, forty-two million followers. It's a number that is honestly so huge I'm physically incapable of comprehending it. I have a simpler definition for what I do: I am a person who found a weird way to make the most boring things seem cool, in sixty seconds or less. I hold up my phone and make videos in which I talk about cheese graters, or juicers, or recipes, and try to tell a short and compelling narrative about it in the best way I can. Sometimes this means I recreate dishes I love; sometimes it means I literally travel across the world to try something that looks delicious. These are all adventures, in one form or another, that I turn into short stories.

This is an inherently quicker and more performed version of myself. It's the social media version of me, but also an expression of the person I am on the inside, let loose in small videos for *a lot of people* to see. In this book, I get to share a different, larger view of myself. I get to share the version of myself my friends and family know and love. I want this book to feel like we're sitting together on lawn chairs by the fire, talking about life. I want to share the deeper stories, to write about where I came from, and what it really is like to have a career in social media. Maybe more than anything, I want to tell you what *I* think of the online version of myself.

It's certainly not a hard job—not compared to the many long and difficult ones I've had before (which you will also learn about in this book). I don't have to wake up early and work two full-time jobs, with no idea how to get out from under them. But at the same time, I want to share the real work that goes into my work, to give an honest view of what it takes for me to be successful. I want to show people that work ethic still matters, even if, and maybe *especially* if, you don't get to see the work.

This book isn't just a memoir, because it is food, I truly believe, that brings us all together. Just like with my videos, I want to leave you with something valuable that you can take home with you and share with other people. These recipes are important tools in how I am able to tell my story and are deeply tied to who I am as a person, and the emotions that accompany my life. This food is a part of me, and it is why this is both cookbook and memoir, giving you lessons about cooking and life.

Because of my unique career path, this cookbook is structured in a different way from most other ones you'll come across. It's not organized by breakfast, appetizers, main courses, and desserts. Instead, this book is a series of short stories about my life, told in chronological order, with each one tied to a recipe that is incredibly important to me. I want it to unfold like a story that highlights the foods I love to cook and eat. While it is designed to be read like an

unfurling narrative, I also want to empower you to skip around. If you want to just read the essays and ignore the food, you can absolutely do that. Or if you don't want to read a story and instead just want to flip to a recipe that looks delicious and put some dinner on the table, you are hereby given the permission to do that too.

At the end of the day, I'm not a chef. I'm just a person who has learned to love cooking, who knows what he likes, and who has worked really hard to figure out how to make food to his taste. With these recipes, I want you to feel like we're in the kitchen cooking together. This book is filled with the dishes I love, designed so that you can truly cook them at home. It is how I cook: making food that gets the most flavor in the fewest steps possible. As you read these recipes, just know that if it has you doing a step, it's because I think the work is absolutely worth the flavor payoff. I sincerely hope these recipes give you the sense of warmth and community that it has given me.

I went from living in my car with no money, to working jobs with no future, to now having met and worked with just about every single one of my celebrity heroes, sharing my stories on the biggest stage I could have ever imagined. I am humbled to tell you that this is my journey and my life, in stories and recipes. This is a book about learning to live in the present, growing as a person, working hard, and then seeing how life unfolds.

"

These recipes are important tools in how I am able to tell my story and are deeply tied to who I am as a person, and the emotions that accompany my life.

"

recipes *and* stories

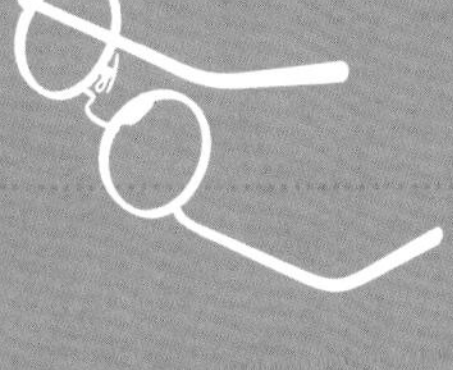

“

My Lela had tons of cookbooks, and when I got older, I opened them up and started to see this whole new world.

”

pineapple upside-down cake is no piece of cake

When I was a kid, I always thought my older brother, Elijah, got way more attention from our family and their friends than I ever did. It felt like my parents were hyper-attentive to Elijah in a way they just weren't with me. In their defense, my parents didn't have a lot of money to do things and were working really hard with two kids. Back then—when I was about ages five to nine—we lived in Victorville, California, and there was just a lot going on for my parents, trying to make ends meet. Because of that, my brother and I would often get dropped off at my great-aunt Tia's house, where there were lots of family and friends around. I remember *everybody* loved my brother. He was cool, and confident, and just naturally drew people to him. I always felt like the addition, or the burden.

I think my grandmother saw that I felt out of place and went out of her way to try to fill that gap for me. Her name was Nikki, but I always called her Lela—a childhood mispronunciation of "abuela" that just stuck. She was this incredibly independent woman, but she would drop all that independence to help me feel special. When my brother and I spent time at her house, he would usually just sit in the other room, drawing, watching movies, or playing video games, while Lela invited me into the kitchen to bake with her.

At the beginning it was just simple things: boxed cakes, brownies, or cookies with simple ingredients. But my Lela had tons of cookbooks, and when I got older, I opened them up and started to see this whole new world. I read through them and fell in love with one particular recipe. I can't remember what the book was anymore, but it was a recipe for pineapple upside-down cake. I was thrilled when she said we could make it together.

Lela had an old oven that didn't work all that well. On our first attempt, I distinctly remember taking it out of the oven and cutting into it . . . and it was just completely raw in the middle. The undercooked batter poured out like hot soup. We tried again and again, but something always went wrong. We couldn't get the pineapples to come out clean on the flip, so we tried more butter. Then we tried nonstick spray, different pan sizes, different temperatures, and different amounts of flour. Months passed, and even when we weren't making it, the cake occupied my mind. I focused on it the way I used to obsess over Batman or Power Rangers. I couldn't wait to get back in the kitchen with my grandmother and try again. We bonded over the failures, with her laughing at me while I dug into underbaked, torn, or collapsed cakes. It was all I could think about. It even began to make me wonder if the all-consuming way I thought about my new hobby was maybe not normal.

Looking back, I can recognize this as the beginning of a pattern that wasn't just work ethic, drive, or passion: I have an obsessive personality that exists to this day. When I can't figure something out, or I'm not good enough at something, or I have a goal I'm trying to reach, it takes over my whole brain.

Now, as a person who's viewed as a success in the social media space, I come across a lot of people who look at my career achievements as a goal and want advice on how to do it themselves. The truth is that there is no sure way to do this, but when I look at my own path, I can't help but think that my obsessive personality is a big reason for it. It is this incredibly powerful driving force in my life, but one that also pains me mentally. My whole life I have had this drive toward obsessions, which would be incredibly intense even if they were short-lived and eventually replaced by something else. They would consume my thoughts and make me fidget unconsciously and constantly. The only thing I've ever found that could level me out from the fidgeting was to actually spend time on the obsession. As a little kid, it was toys, and then it turned into this cake with my grandmother. As a teenager, my obsession was wrestling. In high school and college, it was baseball. Now it is working as a creator in social media, where it's the primary thing I think about every single day.

I want to stress that I'm not saying my job is hard. But success for me has always sort of come as a byproduct of my obsessions.

Some friends or family will call my devotion work ethic, but I think of work ethic as something goal-oriented. Obsession is a goal that you can never quite satisfy. If you reach the goal post, then the goal post immediately moves back. My obsessions feel just as important as eating or breathing. Maybe even more sometimes.

Does that mean that this work-life balance is sustainable or healthy? I don't know. (My friends and family will probably say no.) But I love the constant nature of my work, and the way it genuinely seems to bring joy, or at least relief or distraction, to millions of people. But more than anything, due to my obsessive nature, I feel the need to keep at it, no matter how drained I feel, or how thinly stretched I might become. They say that content is a beast that needs to be constantly fed, so maybe that's why it works so well for me. To be honest, at this moment, this trait of mine feels like a superpower that I can take advantage of, even if I know that at some point, I will have to come to terms with the repercussions, and learn how to harness it for my own long-term mental health.

So now, when I think back to making the pineapple upside-down cake with my grandmother, I remember the first time we ever made it: me, just a kid, looking at all the grocery store ingredients scattered on a table. I couldn't believe that these various things, mixed together in the right amount and in the right order, could be poured into a container and placed in an oven . . . and then come out as a cake. It looked perfect . . . right up until the knife went in, and the undercooked batter poured out. I ate it with a spoon, and I remember to this day my Lela howling with laughter and asking, "Why are you eating it?"

"It's still cake," I said.

We never perfected it together. After she passed back in 2021, I didn't make the cake again—until I started writing this book and broke out the pineapples and maraschinos. When I recreated it, the memories of the person who brought me joy, especially in my failures, came flooding back. I was afraid it would make me sad, but the truth was, it just made me think my grandmother is out there somewhere, getting such a kick out of me having my own cookbook. I hope this recipe does her proud. I hope you try it too. Even if it isn't perfect, it doesn't actually matter. Because working on it, as I learned from her, was always the best part anyway.

PREP TIME: 15 MINUTES COOK TIME: 50 MINUTES, PLUS 15 MINUTES RESTING TIME SERVES 8–10

GRANDMA'S PINEAPPLE UPSIDE-DOWN CAKE

- 1 stick salted butter
- ⅔ cup tightly packed light or dark brown sugar
- 9 pineapple rings from a 20oz (567g) can, drained
- 9 maraschino cherries, stems removed (optional)
- 1⅓ cups all-purpose flour
- 1 cup granulated white sugar
- ¾ cup whole milk
- ⅓ cup vegetable shortening
- 1 egg
- 1½ tsp baking powder
- ½ tsp fine sea salt

1. Preheat the oven to 350°F (180°C).
2. In a 9 x 9-inch (23 x 23cm) metal pan, add the butter and place in the oven. Once the butter is melted and bubbling, remove the pan from the oven and tilt to coat the bottom and sides. On the bottom of the pan, sprinkle the brown sugar evenly over the butter, then arrange the pineapple slices in a single layer. Arrange the cherries (if using) in the center of each pineapple.
3. In a medium bowl using an electric hand mixer or in the bowl of a stand mixer fitted with the whisk attachment, add the flour, white sugar, milk, shortening, egg, baking powder, and salt. Mix on low speed for 30 seconds, scraping the sides as needed. Gradually increase the speed to high, beating for 3 minutes more and scraping the sides frequently. Pour the batter over the pineapple (and cherries, if using), then transfer the pan to the center of the oven.
4. Bake for 50 to 55 minutes, until a toothpick inserted in the center of the cake comes out clean. Remove from the oven and place a heatproof plate upside-down on top of the cake. Immediately flip the plate and cake over and let it sit for at least 10 minutes, or up to 20 minutes. The goal is to let it set and caramelize while still staying warm.
5. Carefully lift the pan and pray for great results. Serve immediately, or cover loosely with plastic or foil to keep warm before serving. Leftovers can be stored in an airtight container in the refrigerator for up to 1 week.

i wasn't good at anything

Being obsessive does not automatically make you good at anything, and when I was a kid, I was horrible at everything. I couldn't dance. I couldn't sing. I couldn't draw. Everyone around me seemed to be good at *something*. Even going into early adolescence, I felt like average was the best I could get at anything. I remember being asked in fifth grade, "What do you want to be when you grow up?" I couldn't answer. My mind was an absolute blank. Other kids would say "astronaut" or "doctor," but those jobs scared me and seemed impossible. Trying to come up with an answer filled me with guilt and anxiety, and the best I could come up with was trying to do what my dad did; I just figured I would grow up and install mailboxes for the rest of my life. But all I really wanted was a purpose in life—to have some kind of life that I could pour my obsessive brain into.

At ten years old, my family moved to Oceanside, just north of San Diego. I was in a new place, trying so hard to find that purpose, eventually turning my focus toward wanting to be a wrestler on TV. I loved watching those matches—the flair, the personalities, the athleticism. I looked up wrestling academies and sent letters to Ohio Valley Wrestling and Florida Championship Wrestling, begging to let me join. I was a skinny kid, yet was fully convinced professional wrestling would be my future. I had absolutely no skills and no true understanding of wrestling, but I poured myself into these letters. I was telling my story, expressing my passion, and I wrote about it with absolute certainty. I didn't even really know how to work out at the time. I was just a kid with a dream. But I would wake up at four or five every morning and try to do a thousand pushups and a thousand crunches before school. I even tried to cut weight by eating less and working out more. I was inventing my own discipline

> "Sometimes the thing you think is your purpose actually serves to teach you something new about yourself."

Florida never bothered to write back. Ohio did, but it was a rejection, and I had to come to terms with the fact that no matter how obsessed I was, I had no idea what else I could do to become a wrestler. I now realize I was developing a skillset that would serve me well as I got older: a combination of hard work, drive, and a thick skin to survive failure.

I truly believe that everyone out there has a valuable skill that just needs to be developed. I think people tend to focus on what they're bad at and ignore the things they're good at, missing their true gifts or not appreciating the ones they already have. But also, sometimes the thing you think is your purpose actually serves to teach you something new about yourself.

Trying every single day to be a wrestler did not turn me into a wrestler. But I think that what I actually loved about wrestling wasn't the wrestling at all, but the *storytelling*. Regardless of what I thought I wanted out of it, it was the mundane day-to-day work that put me on the path to self-discovery.

TOTAL TIME: **5 MINUTES** SERVES **1**

Hard work can be like a big glass of green juice: It's good for you, whether or not you want to drink it. But you also can't be too hard on yourself, and that's why it's okay to have a little sugar with your medicine to keep you coming back for more. That sentiment is the basis for this easy recipe for a Sweet-Enough Apple Green Juice, in which you take store-bought apple juice and infuse it with way more nutrition. I make this just for myself, but this recipe is adaptable: Simply multiply it for a bigger batch. And for extra fiber, you can drink it without straining. Do I want to drink spinach and ginger and turmeric every morning? Heck no. But some apple juice goes a long way to making this into a delicious, nutritious morning routine that helps me keep going. Just keep in mind: Turmeric can stain—so omit it if you're worried about staining your blender with a bit of yellow.

SWEET-ENOUGH APPLE GREEN JUICE

1 cup clear apple juice, or to your preference
1 cup loosely packed baby spinach leaves
1 ice cube
½in (1cm) knob of fresh ginger, peeled
½in (1cm) knob of fresh turmeric, peeled, or 1 tsp ground turmeric

1. In a blender, place the apple juice, spinach, ice, ginger, and turmeric. Blend until completely smooth.
2. Pour the liquid through a fine-mesh strainer and into a glass, stirring the liquid in the strainer with a spoon as you go to help the juice get through. Strain until only solids remain, discard the solids, and enjoy.

fear of rejection

From a young age, I was very aware of my parents' financial troubles. They never explicitly stated it, but my dad had this big old savings jar of quarters, nickels, and dimes. Whenever we had a field trip or an activity, the other kids would show up with one-, five-, or even ten-dollar bills. But for my brother and me, if we got any money at all, we'd walk up with our pockets weighed down with loose change. When we would bring up something that required financial assistance, we could tell it was this giant cause of stress. So for the longest time, I just stopped asking for things that cost money. Most things in life seemed so completely tied to money, and asking for help felt like it was too much of a burden.

In the rare instance where I needed or wanted something badly enough to ask, I was completely strangled by fear and nervousness. "Mom . . . is it possible . . . that you could possibly . . . " I would start to say, and she would cut me off. "If you want something, just ask," she told me. She wanted to teach me that *how* you ask matters more than *what* you ask. The idea of asking for help felt so foreign to me and was so enmeshed with stress and finance that it took some time for me to learn that asking with confidence matters. "It's better to just be confident in what you want," she told me. "When you're confident, people go with it and assume you know what you're talking about."

After I ran out of ideas and it seemed that wrestling was not in my future, my brain became desperate to find its next obsession, and my attention turned to football. Maybe it was because my dad loved watching them, but I saw football players as these beloved figures. For a kid who felt so constantly rejected, football players seemed like they had the greatest lives in the world. They were wanted. They were

A baby picture of me that captures me exactly how I am: always just going with the flow. I was a pretty relaxed baby. I really liked cookie dough and I didn't cry much.

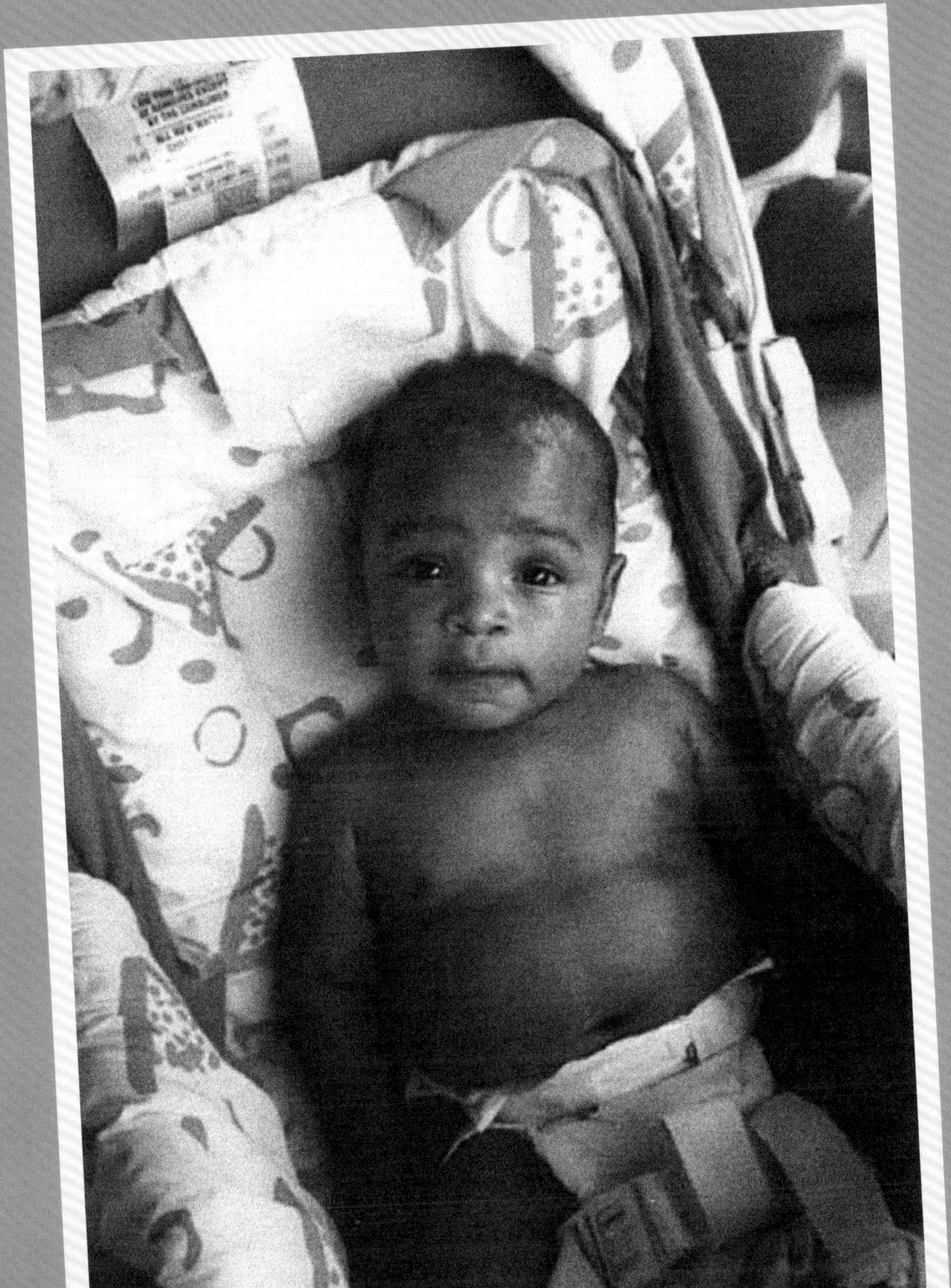

“

What I really wanted had little to do with playing football. It was about attention, but also about what being a football player represented: a path to supporting my family.

”

popular. They were cool, and I was the opposite of cool—an awkward kid in hand-me-down clothes, getting made fun of for eating "hot dog burritos," which were literally just hot dogs wrapped up in tortillas and stuffed into reused oversize ziplock bags.

What I really wanted had little to do with playing football. It was about attention, but also about what being a football player *represented*: a path to supporting my family. I wanted so badly to ease my parents' financial burden. I dreamed of a future of scholarships and the NFL draft and that first payday, when I could ease the weight they'd been shouldering my whole damn life.

This was another chapter in my life when I did not find my true calling, but one in which the attempt to find it put me on the right path. One of the skills I needed so badly to develop was learning how to ask for help, for support, for collaboration, to speak up for what I needed. I knew how to work hard, but without help and guidance, a lot of that hard work would easily turn into wasted energy.

These kinds of lessons and memories frequently remind me of my mom. Because of her, I grew up on sweet grits, and I still love them to this day. Every Saturday morning, she made breakfast for our family. We would still be in our pajamas, watching a movie or cartoons, and I could smell the aromas of that perfect breakfast wafting in from the kitchen. Bacon would be sizzling and popping in the skillet, eggs would be frying away, toast would pop out of the toaster, and best of all: slow-cooked corn grits were ladled into bowls, sprinkled with cinnamon sugar, and topped with a fat pat of butter that quickly melted. But as an adult, whenever I ordered sweet corn grits at a restaurant or talked about them online, I found that a lot of people *hate* sweet grits and think grits are only supposed to be savory. It got to the point where I was embarrassed asking for sweet grits instead of the more common savory kind, afraid someone was going to say, "Oh my God, what is wrong with you?!" But then I remembered my mom's advice, and it turns out that if you speak up and just say it confidently, not only will they happily give them to you, but other people might hear that confidence and think, "Wow. You know what? Sweet grits sound pretty good."

PREP TIME: **1 MINUTE** COOK TIME: **10 MINUTES** SERVES **2**

QUICK SWEET GRITS WITH SALTED BUTTER AND CINNAMON SUGAR

½ cup granulated white sugar
1 tbsp dark or light brown sugar
1 tbsp cinnamon
Fine sea salt, to taste
Two 1oz (28g) packets of instant grits
2 tbsp salted butter, plus 2 thin slices for serving

1. In a medium bowl, combine the white sugar, brown sugar, cinnamon, and salt. Whisk until fully combined. Transfer to a container (see note).
2. To a small pot over high heat, add 1 cup water, the grits, and the salted butter and stir. Once the water comes to a boil, turn off the heat. Season the grits with salt and the cinnamon-sugar mixture to taste, starting with 1 teaspoon of the sugar at a time.
3. Transfer the grits to two bowls, then lay a thin slice of butter on top of each, and garnish with an additional sprinkle of cinnamon sugar. Leftovers can be stored in an airtight container in the refrigerator for up to 5 days and served reheated.

Note: The cinnamon-sugar mix yields about ½ cup, so you'll have plenty left over. Use it on anything from oatmeal to buttered toast or even in a cup of coffee. It'll keep indefinitely when stored in an airtight container in the pantry or in a cool, dry place.

“

You don’t see the real work that goes into becoming an icon, or the luck or circumstances involved. You just see the outcome.

”

what is a role model?

I remember a day in high school when I was about fifteen or sixteen years old, and it was after lunch, near the end of the school day. We students were all tired and down, watching the clock in the classroom. That day, we had a substitute teacher who was probably trying to shake things up when she asked the class to take out a paper and pen and answer the question, "Who is your role model?" I specifically recall thinking that I didn't know what she meant. Was a role model someone I looked up to? Or was it somebody who represented what I wanted to be when I grew up? Were you supposed to mirror their life or follow their rules and morals? I felt like I was supposed to say my dad, so I did. I answered out of fear, which made sense because that was a feeling I always associated with my dad. He had this innate ability to make his presence known: a hulking, muscular being who said the quiet parts out loud. "I should be the most terrifying person in your life," he would say. "If you can handle being afraid of me, you don't have to be afraid of anyone else."

I don't know if it was the best method, because there I was, trying to answer a question in class while thinking about my dad, scared simply by association. For most of my childhood, he had me so afraid of him that breaking a rule was absolutely unthinkable. I was the kid who never snuck out, never talked back, never rebelled—nothing. One time, a family friend spilled a teaspoon of peanut butter on the floor of our home, and when my dad asked who'd done it, they never admitted it was them. My dad punished all of us. For years, just the idea of doing anything somewhat against the grain affected me so deeply. The anxiety around it was crippling. My chest would tighten, my heart would speed up, and my extremities would go cold. I always felt like I was waiting for the other shoe to drop.

But somehow for my brother, born three years before me, it had the opposite effect. As is usually the case, the older sibling gets in trouble while the younger one watches and takes notes. And while we fit that mold to some degree, with my wild brother being the guinea pig and getting disciplined all the time, my father's presence never seemed to have the same anxiety-inducing effect on him. The irony is that my dad was so much more of a role model for my brother than he was for me. My dad didn't live his life with fear. He was a musician, and a very good one. My brother went on to become a very good musician too. I can see a straight line between their paths. How did the same dad raise such different kids?

But what is a role model? I used to think about that question all the time, feeling very confused. So often it's just a title thrust onto famous people. You can dream of being a professional athlete when you grow up and say Kobe Bryant or LeBron James or Michael Jordan are your role models, but that's not really a role model. Those are examples of success, not a path to success. You don't see the real work that goes into becoming an icon, or the luck or circumstances involved. You just see the outcome, the guy on the jumbotron, in the commercials, or winning the championship. A role model, by definition, is someone who models behavior that you want to learn and who you use as an example. But it's hard to model yourself after somebody who is already successful, *especially* when they're a public figure who presents themself in ways that are best for them.

As someone who makes a living on social media, I see this a lot. People present themselves in ways they think will suit their purposes. Videos are edited, filters are added, tone and intention evolve to fit what the algorithm decides will reach more people. The display of emotions and reactions from creators are calibrated to fit a desired presentation.

The truth is that our parents or parental figures are always going to end up being our role models. What they do will always impact us more than what they say. They teach us to be like them or not like them. It turns out that my dad set me up for success way more than a football player or a pro wrestler ever could have.

When I was a kid, just like most kids, I really thought I knew what I wanted and how I felt about everything. Even something as simple as meatloaf night felt like an obstacle I had to overcome. I had this idea in my head that it was gross—I mean, it's a *loaf* of *meat*—and I would choke down as much as I had to but would never finish my meal. I hated that I *had* to eat it. Then one day, I can't even tell you when or why, something changed. I looked at this dense, cake-like structure with charred, crispy edges and a smoky-BBQ-sauce glaze that glistened across the exterior and decided to open up my mind and give it a real chance. With reset expectations and one big bite after another, I not only appreciated it, but I *loved* it. Our parents are our true de facto role models. But since they're our parents, sometimes even when they show us something that is *so obviously true* to everyone else in the world—like how meatloaf is delicious—it takes a little time to submit and accept that they're right.

This photo of my parents, my cousin Jessica, my brother, and me was taken during a family reunion at my tio's house. I fell in the pool that night.

I make this American comfort-food classic at home now to pay my respects to my mom's version, laying it onto a baking sheet, then adding broccoli florets to roast alongside the loaf. I love the way the glaze and meat drippings seep into the broccoli, creating a delicious, nutritious dish, all on one pan.

→

PREP TIME: 20 MINUTES, PLUS 20 MINUTES–24 HOURS RESTING TIME COOK TIME: 1 HOUR TO 1 HOUR 30 MINUTES SERVES 4

GLAZED BEEF MEATLOAF WITH ROASTED BROCCOLI

- 3 slices of white bread, crusts removed, cubed
- ½ cup whole milk
- 3 stalks of celery, roughly chopped
- 2 medium carrots, roughly chopped
- ½ yellow or white onion, roughly chopped
- 1 bunch of flat-leaf Italian parsley, stems removed, roughly chopped (1½ cups, loosely packed)
- 1 tbsp dried oregano leaves
- 1 tbsp granulated garlic
- 1 egg
- ½ tbsp fine sea salt, plus more to taste
- Freshly ground black pepper
- 1lb (450g) 80% lean ground beef
- Olive oil
- 6 tbsp ketchup
- 3 tbsp apple cider vinegar
- 2 tbsp tightly packed brown sugar
- 2 tsp tomato paste
- ½ tbsp soy sauce
- ½ tsp liquid smoke (optional)
- 1 large or 2 medium heads of broccoli, broken into large florets

1. In a large mixing bowl, combine the bread cubes and milk, and toss to combine. Let the mixture sit for 5 minutes, or until the milk is fully absorbed, then break the bread up with your fingers into a crumble.
2. To the bowl of a food processor, add the celery, carrots, onion, and parsley. Pulse until a paste forms. Alternatively, you can use a knife and chop the veggies until very fine.
3. To the bowl with the bread mixture, add the vegetable mixture, along with the oregano, garlic, egg, salt, and several twists of freshly ground black pepper. Mix until thoroughly combined. Add the ground beef and mix until the beef is fully incorporated.
4. To a lightly oiled 9 x 5-inch (23 x 12cm) loaf pan, add the beef mixture and press down to form a flat surface on top, tapping the pan occasionally to remove any air bubbles. Transfer the meatloaf to the refrigerator and chill, covered, for at least 20 minutes and up to a full day, to help it set into its shape.
5. Preheat the oven to 350°F (180°C). Remove the meatloaf from the refrigerator and invert it onto a baking sheet. Shake the sheet until the loaf falls down onto it. If the loaf falls apart at all, don't worry. Just use your hands to reform. Drizzle some olive oil on top of the meatloaf, then bake for 15 minutes.
6. Meanwhile, make the glaze: In a medium mixing bowl, combine the ketchup, vinegar, brown sugar, tomato paste, soy sauce, liquid smoke (if using), and several twists of black pepper. Whisk until thoroughly combined.
7. After the 15 minutes of baking, once the meat has begun to set and the raw color is cooked off, brush a generous amount of the glaze all over the meatloaf. Return it to the oven and bake for another 10 minutes.
8. Meanwhile, in a large mixing bowl, toss the broccoli florets with a pinch of salt and lightly coat with olive oil.
9. Once the 10 minutes are up, open the oven and glaze the meatloaf again, then scatter the broccoli around the edges of the loaf.
10. Return the pan to the oven and bake for 45 to 60 minutes, checking every 15 minutes and glazing the meatloaf each time, until the meatloaf registers an internal temperature of 160°F (70°C) in the thickest part.
11. Remove the pan from the oven and let the meatloaf rest for 10 minutes. Cut it into slices and serve alongside the roasted broccoli. Leftovers can be stored in an airtight container in the refrigerator for up to 6 days.

investing in a pair of pants

My dad loved football. He loved the intense contact of it, of these giant men with the strength of eighteen-wheelers smashing into each other. The power is what drew my dad to the sport but also why he expressly forbade me from playing it. Somehow this made me want to be a football player—the conflicting combination of wanting his approval and *also*, for the first time, expressing something approaching an act of rebellion.

My rebellion didn't last long, but not for the reason you probably expect. I was at my high school looking for the football coach, ready to engage in my big display of disobedience against my father. I saw this bald man who looked every bit the part of a football coach and told him I was interested in joining the team. He gestured out to the baseball field. I was gullible but also an absolute people pleaser at my core. So rather than ask any questions, I just literally thought, "Wow, they're all wearing baseball gear. The football players sure do play a lot of different sports."

A few minutes later, it became extremely obvious that I was trying out for the baseball team. But again, being a people pleaser, I didn't say anything. I just played. Let me tell you, I was *so* incredibly awful at it. Just truly terrible. I couldn't run, couldn't hit, and couldn't field. Despite the fact that I didn't know how to do anything, something clicked in my head after that. I told myself I wanted to be a professional baseball player.

Maybe it was because I *didn't* choose football, or maybe he could see how serious I was about it, but when I told my dad I wanted to be a baseball player, he totally supported me. I said I needed baseball pants and a glove, and he told me to choose *one*, because that was all we could afford. I figured I was a big kid and it would be harder to find a used pair of pants that fit than it would a glove, so I picked the pants.

We got them and I remember it distinctly: The next morning, he dropped me off at school, the air crisp in my lungs. My senses were heightened. In my mind, I was already fully committed to playing baseball, but I had to forge that commitment with fire. I didn't want to let myself down, and I certainly didn't want to let down my father, who spent real money on this dream of mine—money we didn't really have.

In a way, I will always be searching for his approval. My dad, for all intents and purposes, was a very broad person. He could move big, heavy objects, and he could make big decisions for our family. But I never saw him do anything in his life with grace or precision *except* for making a fried egg sandwich. Whenever he got in the kitchen and made breakfast sandwiches for us, he moved with refinement and agility, delicately toasting the bread and frying the eggs so the whites were set and the yolks had a touch of runniness. This was always my ideal sandwich balance: cold, crisp lettuce, a melted slice of American cheese, a crisscross of crispy bacon, a touch of mayo, and that egg, all nestled between two slices of toasted grocery-store sandwich bread. How did a man who could throw a boulder make this aesthetically pleasing breakfast sandwich? It was like magic.

So this is my ode to his perfect sandwich, recreated as best I can, reminding myself that even the biggest, scariest people can make beautiful, elegant things.

PREP TIME: 1 MINUTE   COOK TIME: 7 MINUTES   MAKES 2

“SEARCHING FOR FATHER’S APPROVAL” FRIED EGG SANDWICH

4 slices of wheat or white bread
2 tbsp salted or unsalted butter
2 eggs
Kosher or fine sea salt
Freshly ground black pepper
¼ tsp granulated garlic
2 tbsp mayo
2 slices of American cheese
2 slices of cooked bacon, halved (optional)
2 crispy slices of iceberg lettuce, shredded

1. Place the bread in the toaster, then set a nonstick skillet over medium heat and add the butter. Once the butter has melted, crack the eggs into the pan, being careful not to break the yolks. Use a high-heat rubber spatula to shape the eggs slightly after they hit the pan, making sure they don’t run across the pan and become wider than your bread.
2. Season the eggs generously with salt, then top with some black pepper and the garlic. Using a lid or a sheet pan, cover the skillet. Allow the eggs to cook for 2½ to 3 minutes, until the whites are just barely set.
3. Meanwhile, when the toast is finished, slather one side of each piece with the mayo.
4. Remove the lid from the skillet, lay one slice of cheese on top of each egg, cover again, and cook for 10 more seconds, until the cheese is melted. Place the eggs on two of the toast pieces.
5. Lay two bacon halves (if using) crisscross on each of the sandwiches. Top with the iceberg lettuce, close the sandwich with the remaining slices of bread, and enjoy.

accepting failure

Now, when I say to you I was bad at baseball, I don't think you're accurately picturing how truly awful I was. For a kid who was *terrified* of failure, this was especially painful for me. In my house, failure was not supported. Failure was tied to discipline. If you failed a test, you were in trouble.

So here I was, this tall, gangly, somewhat athletic kid who was smart enough but had absolutely no clue what to do in an organized sports setting. I remember the first thing they had me do was play catch—the most basic thing in the world, and I was doing it wrong, catching the ball with my palm instead of the pocket of the glove. It hurt so much, I thought that when I took my glove off, my hand would be covered in blood.

We also did PFPs, or "pitcher fielding practice." I was supposed to simulate being a batter and run to first base so the pitcher could practice jogging over to first, tossing the ball underhand, and throwing me out. All I had to do was run in a straight line, but I ran to the wrong side of the base and almost got my head knocked off by the ball. I couldn't catch, I couldn't run, and I wasn't great at throwing, either.

To be honest, I don't even think they knew I was trying to join the team. After practice, nobody said, "Good job" or "Keep at it." They just walked off the field like I wasn't there. So I went to the batting cages and tried to learn how to hit. I was in there just swinging away and thinking to myself, "I can only get better from here." Everybody saw me fail, and I was okay with it. Failure, this thing I was so terrified of, had happened to me in a deeply public way already. It was liberating. All I had to do was keep trying, dedicate myself to more practices, more throws, more at-bats, more of everything. I told

My first game being on the freshman/sophomore baseball team at Oceanside in 2013. I didn't play in this game, but it was my first time experiencing what it meant to be part of a team.

“

I hated failure because I hadn’t found the right way to fail.

”

myself: I'm going to get *better* at this. It was my introduction to failure without punishment. There were no real repercussions. You failed? So what? Now you get to do it again, and again, and again. Up until then, I hated failure because I hadn't found the right way to fail.

It turns out that baseball is the perfect place for failure. If you fail seven times out of ten as a batter, you're in the Hall of Fame (a .300 batting average in Major League Baseball is considered very good). If you shoot that percentage on a basketball court, or throw that percentage on a football field, you're *done*. Maybe that's why I love cooking so much: It doesn't have to be perfect for it to still be dinner. You can eat it, be nourished, and think about how you might want to do it differently next time. For example, I hated every pickle I'd ever had . . . until I found fried pickles. It turns out that if you double-bread them in flour, egg, and seasoned breadcrumbs (for an extra crunchy exterior), they're delicious. But I didn't discover this until I tried them at a restaurant and was intrigued enough to develop my own version. I found out that I can take something I don't like and turn it into something I actually enjoy.

While some people swear by using seasoned panko breadcrumbs for that airy crunch, I realized after some trial and error that by using a combination of seasoned panko breadcrumbs *and* cornmeal, you get maximum crunch and the added touch of that southern-fry flavor. Since a lot of people like some spice with their fried pickles, I serve these up with a simple buffalo-ranch dipping sauce, but you can definitely just serve these with a bottle of good old-fashioned ranch dressing and have incredible results.

PREP TIME: 25 MINUTES, PLUS 1-24 HOURS RESTING TIME COOK TIME: 20 MINUTES MAKES 24

THE ONLY PICKLES I'LL EVER EAT (FRIED, WITH BUFFALO RANCH)

½ cup all-purpose flour
1 cup cornmeal, divided
Kosher or fine sea salt
Freshly ground black pepper
8oz (225g) panko breadcrumbs
1 tbsp smoked paprika
1 tbsp granulated garlic
1 tbsp Italian seasoning
4 eggs
3 large whole dill pickles, quartered lengthwise, then halved
1 cup sour cream
1 cup mayo
3 tbsp Frank's RedHot Original Cayenne Pepper Sauce
1oz (28g) packet of ranch-dressing powder
Fry oil, such as canola or peanut

1. Set up your breading station: To a wide bowl, add the flour, half the cornmeal, a generous pinch of salt, and several twists of ground black pepper, and whisk until well combined. To another wide bowl, add the remaining cornmeal, a pinch of salt, more black pepper, and the panko, paprika, granulated garlic, and Italian seasoning, and whisk until well combined. In a third wide bowl, crack the eggs and add 2 tablespoons water, then whisk until fully combined.
2. Line up your components for easy access: the pickles, flour mixture, egg mixture, breadcrumb mixture, and finally, a baking sheet. Using the wet hand–dry hand method (designating one hand for wet ingredients and one for dry), use your dry hand to lay the first pickle in the flour mixture. Flip it over until fully coated. Shake off the excess flour, then lay it in the egg mixture. Use your wet hand to fully coat with the egg. Lift and let the excess egg drain off, then transfer to the panko mixture. Use your dry hand again to dredge in the breadcrumbs, patting slightly to adhere. Dip the pickle back into the egg mixture, then once more in the panko to create a double crust. Lay the spear carefully on the baking sheet and repeat with the remaining pickles.
3. Transfer the pickles to the refrigerator to chill for at least 1 hour and up to a full day to help the breading adhere. (You can skip this step if you're in a hurry, but this helps to keep the pickle from sliding out of its deep-fried shell).
4. Meanwhile, make the dipping sauce: In a medium bowl, combine the sour cream, mayo, hot sauce, and ranch powder. Whisk until thoroughly combined and set aside. (The sauce will keep in the refrigerator for up to 1 week.)
5. When you are ready to cook, set up a deep fryer or a deep, heavy-bottomed pot, like a Dutch oven, on the stove and fill with enough fry oil to comfortably fit the pickles, leaving at least 2 inches (5cm) of space from the surface of the oil to the top of the pot to prevent anything from boiling over.
6. Heat the oil to 350°F (180°C). Fry the pickles for about 2 minutes, being careful not to crowd the pot and working in batches if needed, until the pickles turn a deep golden brown, then transfer them to a paper towel–lined tray. Repeat with the remaining pickles, making sure to return the oil to 350°F (180°C) before adding the next batch.
7. Let cool slightly, then serve with the buffalo-ranch sauce.

being your own support system

I did get to keep practicing, but that didn't mean I got better right away—and people certainly let me know it. Sometimes I was within earshot of players or coaches who maybe didn't know I could hear them, and I would really clearly hear them say how bad I was. But in case that wasn't enough, sometimes they would tell me to my face too. I remember sharing with a coach that my goal was to play Division 1 college baseball. He told me, "If you work really, really hard—the hardest you've ever worked at anything in your life—you have a chance to be on a junior college team. Maybe." This was from my coach, my supposed mentor, and a person I was supposed to *look up to*. These people are often secondary parental figures, and he told me I was dreaming too big.

These encounters shattered my confidence and tore me down to almost nothing. My whole life, I was raised to listen to my elders and to believe that what they say goes. If they're right, then what does that mean for me? Do I just agree with them and admit I have this ceiling, that *they* know how far I can go?

Instead, I had to believe that they could be wrong, and they could have egos and faults, just like us kids. I knew I couldn't look to them for motivation, that I needed to build myself up instead. So, I turned elsewhere. I started watching motivational speakers like Les Brown and Eric Thomas. As the coaches wore down my confidence every day, I would lean on these men's speeches and their philosophies to build me back up. Motivation is like food. If you eat once, you're good for a few hours, but then the battery drains and you need to feed yourself again. To re-up on that motivation, I would download those videos onto my iPod and feast on their speeches, their words, during

"Motivation is like food. If you eat once, you're good for a few hours, but then the battery drains and you need to feed yourself again."

my last two periods of school. All of a sudden, I didn't have to rely on other people in my life. I learned how to be my own support system. It all came down to a change in perspective: I didn't like what the people around me were saying to me, so I had to find words from somebody else. It proved to me that it didn't matter if they were saying it to me *specifically*. Complete strangers on a recording made me feel better than the supposed coaches who were around me in my life. I didn't like the version of "support" I was presented with, so I changed the narrative and it allowed me to change my approach.

PREP TIME: 15 MINUTES COOK TIME: 10 MINUTES MAKES ABOUT 8

I may not have had coaches who I thought believed in me, but I still wanted to achieve what they did not see for me. Well, I like to imagine that there are apples out there that are dying to become donuts, and they just need someone to believe. For this recipe, I am that coach who believes in them. I cut these apples into rings, batter them, fry them, and dust them in cinnamon sugar. I help these apples become donuts, and with this recipe, now you can too.

APPLE DONUTS

- 2 large apples, such as Cosmic Crisp or Red Delicious
- 1 cup all-purpose flour
- 1 tbsp granulated white sugar
- ¼ tsp baking powder
- ¾ cup almond or whole milk
- Fry oil, such as canola or avocado oil
- 1 batch cinnamon sugar (see page 32)

1. The goal here is to cut your apples into rings that are shaped like donuts. Turn each apple on its side and cut it into roughly ½-inch-thick (1cm) slices through the core. Next, use a plastic bottle cap or a very small cookie cutter to cut through the core of each slice. Set aside.
2. In a large mixing bowl, combine the flour, sugar, and baking powder, and whisk to combine. Pour in the milk and whisk to form a pancake-like batter.
3. In a deep-fryer, deep skillet, or Dutch oven, add about 2 inches (5cm) of fry oil and heat, keeping the temperature between 350°F and 375°F (180°C and 190°C). Set up a paper towel–lined plate or a wire rack over a sheet pan. Pour the cinnamon sugar into a wide bowl.
4. Working one by one, drop an apple slice into the batter. Once fully coated, use tongs to lift it out and allow the excess batter to drip off before carefully transferring to the fry oil. Fry for 45 seconds to 1 minute on each side, until it has a golden- to medium-brown color, similar to an apple-cider donut.
5. Using a slotted spoon or clean tongs, transfer the fried apple to the prepared plate or wire rack to drain the excess oil.
6. While still hot, move the donut to the bowl of cinnamon sugar and fully coat. Transfer to a plate and repeat the batter and fry process with the remaining donuts. Serve while still warm.

taking the leap

I never wanted to go to college until baseball came into play. In my mind, college meant debt, so the thought of going wasn't on my mind at first. Ever since I was a kid, I figured I would just get my high school diploma and immediately enter the workforce. Why put my family in debt when I could make money instead? I'd never heard of the ACTs or SATs, until I took them last minute, without studying. I had never been told about financial aid. These all seemed like things that mattered for everybody else.

In high school, baseball took over my life. I had identified strength as the area in which I could get better without needing my coaches or really anyone else to be able to make improvements. I put together a strict regimen for myself for a full year: two weeks of high-weight and low-rep weight training, followed by two weeks of low weight and high reps. Squatting, bench press, back, abs, triceps, plank holds, toe raises—the full cycle, with two weeks of one and two weeks of the other, over and over again. I also hit three hundred balls per day off a tee in the batting cages, focusing on power and accuracy. Then for three meals a day, I ate the same thing: one cup of brown rice, one cup of steamed broccoli, and three chicken breasts along with gallons of water, and then I would sleep for twelve hours. Looking back, the craziest part is that the food was purely fuel. I didn't even season the *nine* chicken breasts I was putting down every day. I simply cooked the frozen chicken breasts—usually not even bothering to defrost them first—and ate them. There was no joy, no pleasure, just conditioning, eating, and sleeping. I wasn't even doing my homework. Within four months, I went from 190 pounds to 230. I was already naturally growing at that age . . . but my growth was still a lot.

My last game of my sophomore year in high school in 2016. This was my first official season playing baseball, and I created such a bond with my teammates that I didn't want the season to end.

PIRATES

Needless to say, baseball was my Plan A, and I didn't have a Plan B. I knew I was a project and not a prodigy, so if I wanted to have any chance of making it as a professional, I needed to find a way to play after high school. I eventually saw the writing on the wall and discovered that this meant college. But as the kid who was working on baseball instead of homework, I now needed to learn how to focus on getting into a college in the same way I had focused on baseball. I was already so far behind on college planning compared to other students, but I submitted applications, talked to advisors, and tried to wrap my head around the sheer money involved in merely going to school. Even *applying* to college was too expensive. I still wasn't getting the in-game reps I was hoping for, and because of that, the Division 1 college team was not in the cards for me right away. Division 1 was the top level of college baseball, but my reality was that I was more likely to go to community college first and then try to transfer to Division 1. Ironically, this was the same path that the one coach had told me about; the one who had insulted me just a few months earlier. Had he been right all along? I was determined to make the situation a stepping stone rather than a death sentence.

At that same time, my best friend ended up getting an academic scholarship award through the Gates Millennium Scholars Program, which paid for his entire four-year college education. I had actually tried to apply to be a scholar too, but couldn't get my application together by the deadline. My friend eventually got accepted into Pepperdine and went on to make the baseball team there. I was unbelievably happy for him, but his success made me look at myself. It was so clear to me that I had put myself in the very position I was in. I realized that working hard at baseball wouldn't be enough; I needed to work hard at the academics and the research too. But I hadn't laid the groundwork early enough, hadn't studied the road to college with enough focus and intelligence, and I was too late. I had worked hard, but not smart. My friend was living my dream, and the only person I had to blame for my situation was myself.

I did catch a break, though. There was a late-afternoon home game, the second to last game of the season. I was a DH (designated hitter, meaning I was just hitting and not playing on the field on

defense). I had four at-bats that game and struck out all four times. One after the other. I was so discouraged, so down on myself, and nobody would look at me or talk to me—either out of embarrassment or politeness, I'm not sure. My dad picked me up after the game, and I didn't tell him what happened. I thought my high school baseball career was over and that they weren't going to play me in the next game. I was sitting on the couch in our living room, wanting to cry but not letting myself, when I got a call from a random number and for some reason decided to answer it.

"Hello, is this Jordan?" the voice boomed. "This is John Welker, and I'm the coach of the College of the Desert."

"What's the college?" I asked.

"College of the Desert," he repeated. I didn't understand that that was the name of a school. I thought he was *describing* it.

My high school coach, amazingly, had put in a good word for me, recommending that I could use more time to grow into the player I wanted to be. For the first time in my life, I felt like someone outside my own family was actually taking a chance on me. I was going to get to work on my skills somewhere. I had somebody who believed in me. I was on the path, as I saw it, to one day playing Division 1 baseball.

PREP TIME: 5 MINUTES, PLUS 20 MINUTES OF COOLING   COOK TIME: 20 MINUTES   MAKES ABOUT 6 CUPS

When I was little, my dad used to make this incredible trail mix, combining sweet and savory into one beautifully balanced blend. Looking back now to the days when I was on the path to becoming a Division 1 baseball player, eating unseasoned chicken breasts, I wish I'd had this trail mix to keep me energized and fueled through those long days with a little more joy. This is my version of my dad's trail mix, with some smoky almonds and cashews that I roast myself. I wish I could give a bag of it to high school Jordan. If you come upon anybody in a similar situation to young me, maybe you'll whip up a batch of this trail mix and help them out with their own journey.

DAD'S TRAIL MIX WITH SMOKED SALT-ROASTED CASHEWS

1½ cups raw almonds
1½ cups raw cashews
1½ tbsp olive oil, coconut oil, or preferred oil
2 tsp smoked flaky salt, such as Maldon, plus more to taste
1 cup dried bananas or banana chips (sweetened or unsweetened, depending on preference)
½ cup dried cranberries
½ cup chocolate chips

1. Preheat the oven to 300°F (150°C). Line a baking sheet with parchment paper.
2. In a large mixing bowl, combine the almonds, cashews, olive oil, and smoked salt. Lay them in a single layer on the prepared baking sheet.
3. Roast in the oven for 20 minutes, stirring and rotating the baking sheet halfway through.
4. Remove the nuts from the oven and let them cool. While still slightly warm, taste them for seasoning and add more salt if desired (it will adhere better if they are still warm). Once completely cool, return the nuts to the mixing bowl and add the bananas, cranberries, and chocolate chips. Toss until well combined and store in a sealed container. It will keep for 1 to 2 months stored in a cool, dry place or for several months in the freezer.

proving everyone wrong

At College of the Desert, down in Palm Desert, California, my physical transformation became even more pronounced. They say that in baseball, there are five skills to master: batting power, batting accuracy, speed, fielding, and throwing. If you excel at them all, you're a hall of famer. If you excel at three, you're a superstar. But even if you are good at just one, you have the potential to find a place in the sport. You don't have to be complete to be a pro. All you need is potential to get drafted into the major leagues. I saw guys "make the league" just because they were incredibly fast runners, and a team figured maybe they could teach them to do something else too.

When I took a step back and looked at those five tools, I asked myself what I could build up and control. Throwing? No, I had a weak arm, and it was too hard to develop that. Speed? I wasn't inherently elite, and it would have taken too long to train up that skillset. Batting average? I wasn't getting enough minutes on the team to really develop that one, either. I needed game time to improve. One thing I did have were fast hands; I could get the bat to the ball quickly. I also knew that I didn't need anybody else's help to hit the weight room. So power was going to continue to be my focus. If I combined bat speed with power? Now we were getting somewhere.

Once again, I focused all my obsessive tendencies toward the weight room, but more specifically to power hitting. I kept at it, adding power every single day. The way I saw it, I had two sources of motivation. In the morning, I motivated myself by dreaming of getting my family out of their financial mess. I wanted to make money, support my parents, and buy them a house. In the evenings, when I pushed heavy weights, I thought about all the people I wanted

Playing for the College of the Desert in 2017, alongside my teammates in the dugout.

“

I had a talent. I was better than everyone else at something. For the first time in my life, I felt like I had a real skill.

”

to prove wrong. I imagined them all sitting on the couch at the end of a long day, relaxing, maybe having a drink. While they did so, I was outworking them. I imagined the people who said I wouldn't make it, and I decided that if you're not doing more than me, then I don't want to hear from you.

There was a moment when I knew it was working. On our practice field, there was this big old tree way back in left field. Ever since the first day of batting practice, everyone would try to hit the ball so hard that it went way back and hit the tree. One day, after I'd spent months of time in the weight room, the pitcher threw a ball toward the inside part of my hip. I swung, and pulled the ball to the left side of the field and hit the top of the tree. I was in shock. That just did not happen. Everyone was stunned. From then on, I kept learning how to use my power. I was roping balls. The coaches all knew now. Everybody knew. I had a talent. I was better than everyone else at something. For the first time in my life, I felt like I had a real skill.

Here's the thing: Some people are undeniable and some things are uncrustable. I know; that's a wild leap, but stay with me. To some people, the crustless little PB&Js are merely an easy snack you don't think much about. They're something you grab that doesn't matter much. I could relate. But then, all of a sudden, you put something else on top, and people notice. You add some muscles, or you dip the thing in egg, milk, and cinnamon, and now everybody is paying attention.

PREP TIME: 3 MINUTES, PLUS 30 MINUTES OF THAWING TIME   COOK TIME: 8 MINUTES   MAKES 4

FRENCH TOAST UNCRUSTABLES

½ cup whole milk
2 eggs
2 tsp vanilla extract
1 tsp ground cinnamon
4 Uncrustables, ideally thawed on the counter for at least 30 minutes
2 tbsp salted butter, plus more as needed
¼ cup powdered sugar, plus more as needed
Maple syrup, to serve

1. Preheat a wide skillet, ideally cast iron, over medium heat or preheat a griddle to 350°F (180°C).
2. To a wide bowl or baking dish, add the milk, eggs, vanilla extract, and cinnamon. Whisk until well combined, then add all four Uncrustables, flipping them over to fully saturate on all sides with the milk mixture.
3. To the skillet or griddle, add the butter. Once foaming and melted, tilt to coat the entire bottom of the skillet. Using tongs, lift the first Uncrustable, allowing the excess batter to drip off. Lay it in the skillet, and repeat with as many as will fit in the skillet. Cook for about 3 minutes, or until the bottoms are golden brown. Flip and repeat on the other side, adding more butter as needed to grease the cooking surface.
4. Once golden brown on both sides, place the Uncrustables on individual plates or on a serving platter. Using a fine-mesh strainer, generously dust the Uncrustables with the powdered sugar.
5. Serve with a side of maple syrup and be very careful because the filling can get extremely hot. I have made this mistake before.

highs and lows: i can almost taste it

With my newfound skill, I was ready to find my way onto a Division 1 baseball team. I kept telling myself that Division 1 didn't mean you were one of the best baseball players in college. I thought about the scholarships I didn't apply for in time in high school and knew I needed to apply my work ethic not just to baseball but also to self-promotion. I would sit in the library after classes at the community college, then message every head coach, assistant coach, and any affiliated coach I could find an email address for. I would send my baseball stats and my grades, writing that I was a 6'2", 230-pound power hitter with great grades and a passion to get better. I sent thirty to forty emails a day, totaling somewhere around twelve hundred emails.

Of those, I heard back from five schools, which was incredibly gratifying in its own right. Ohio State offered me a fall roster spot, which was essentially an elongated tryout. But one of the other schools who'd responded was UC Riverside, which had just recently been placed in Division 1. I also had some family that had gone there, and it was relatively close to my home in Oceanside. The coach at Riverside told me there was a real chance I would not make the team, but I said I didn't need any guarantees. I showed up for training camp, and once again put in the work. And I made the team. It was a seven-year journey, after everyone told me it would be impossible. I was on a Division 1 baseball team. Coach told me that I made the team because of my potential, but also because of my character and the level of kindness I exuded not just to my teammates, but to the coaches, staff, janitors—everybody.

I was riding high. I made the team. But I was also deep in debt. I couldn't afford college, naively hoping I would receive some kind of scholarship. But then one day, I opened up my accounts and saw that all my school debts were paid. Nobody said anything to me, and I had no idea who to thank. It was just a mysterious benefactor who maybe heard my story and took care of it. To this day, I have no idea who helped me out.

It seemed like everything was finally going my way. But highs in life are often followed by lows. Not long after that, I discovered a very weird loophole at UC Riverside that has since been reversed. Essentially, I had passed *too many classes* in community college, so I was allowed to be on the team at Riverside, but I wasn't allowed to play in any games. It was almost like a redshirt year, but it wasn't a redshirt. It was just a dumb administrative rule. I had a year to wait out on the team, leaving me with one year left of eligibility for my senior season. It was an emotional roller coaster of time for me.

Later that year—I was twenty-two years old at this point—in the last summer before my senior season, a scout for the Arizona Diamondbacks named Jeremiah Luster, a former major league baseball player who was from Oceanside too, reached out to me over text. We'd casually met in passing back in high school when I was just sixteen, and I think he saw me as a local kid with a tough upbringing he wanted to keep tabs on. He had been watching our practices and got my number from our coach. He told me that there were a handful of teams that would be interested in drafting me if I could develop a few skills and hit a few benchmarks next season. He gave me the kind of advice nobody else in my life could have, and it meant the world to me. The list of goals he gave me was *attainable*. I thought, "Oh my God, I might actually get drafted."

I could see my success. I could *smell* it. This was my big chance.

To me, the sweet smell of success has the aroma of a big, juicy cheeseburger. I can smell the beef fat sizzling and the bacon rendering. I can almost taste it. If making the majors was a cheeseburger, it would be this one: an all-beef patty seared in a hot skillet, served with hickory bacon, a thick slice of seared white onion, a melted piece of Colby jack, and a hunk of iceberg lettuce on a sesame brioche bun.

PREP TIME: **10 MINUTES** COOK TIME: **30 MINUTES** MAKES **4**

GRILLED ONION-BACON CHEESEBURGER

- 1½lb (675g) 80% lean ground beef, divided into 4 equal portions
- 4 slices of hickory bacon
- 5 tbsp salted butter, divided
- ½ large white onion, cut into slices
- 4 hamburger buns, preferably sesame brioche
- Mayo
- Yellow mustard
- Kosher or fine sea salt
- Freshly ground black pepper
- 2 tsp granulated onion
- 2 tsp granulated garlic
- 4 slices Colby jack
- 4 hand-torn slices of iceberg lettuce

1. Shape your ground beef into patties. The trick here is to handle them as little as possible (the more you work the patty, the tougher the meat will become). Place the beef directly on a plate or sheet pan and use your hands to form the beef gently into very loosely packed patties that are slightly wider than your hamburger buns. Place in the refrigerator to chill while you get everything else ready.
2. Lay the bacon in a 12-inch (30cm) cast-iron skillet and set it over medium-high heat. Once the bacon starts to sizzle in the pan, allow it to render and cook for about 5 minutes, flipping occasionally, until it has taken on some mahogany coloring and is crispy at the edges with a little bit of chewiness left. Transfer it to a paper towel–lined plate and set aside. Wipe the fat from the pan with a paper towel and throw the towel away.
3. To the same pan, add 1 tablespoon of the butter. Once melted, tilt the pan to spread the butter, then add the onion in an even layer, pressing down with a spatula to get as much contact with the pan as you can. Sear the onions for about 3 minutes, leaving them untouched until they are lightly browned. Give them a quick stir and then let them cook for about 1 minute more, or until they take on more color and are softened but not mushy. Lift the onions out and transfer to a plate.
4. Toast the buns, cut-side down, in the skillet for about 30 seconds each, working in batches until they're lightly golden brown, then transfer to a plate or a clean surface, cut-side up.
5. Spread the top buns with mayo and the bottom buns with mustard.
6. Set the same skillet over high heat. Take the burgers out of the fridge. Season the tops of the patties liberally with an even sprinkling of salt, freshly ground black pepper, and half the granulated onion and garlic. Add 2 tablespoons of the butter to the skillet. When melted, lay the first two patties, seasoned-side down, into the skillet. Season the other side with more salt and pepper and half of the remaining granulated onion and garlic. Let cook for 2 to 3 minutes, untouched, until a nice crust has formed.
7. Use a spatula to flip the burgers, then lay a slice of cheese on top of each, followed by half of the grilled onions. Snap the bacon in half and crisscross it on top. Continue cooking the burger to your preferred doneness. I prefer medium-well, which is usually 2 to 3 minutes more. If you use an instant-read thermometer, look for an internal temperature of about 150°F (66°C). Lay the iceberg lettuce on the bottom buns, then place the burger on top, close the bun, and serve immediately.
8. Repeat with the remaining two burgers, and enjoy.

. . . and then it wasn't

At the beginning of my senior season, I sat down with my coach. I told him I had a chance to get drafted, and I wanted an honest chance to prove myself. I made a declaration. This was my shot.

I had been working out as hard as I possibly could. I was fighting for playing time. As all of this was going on, my grandmother—the one who taught me how to make pineapple upside-down cake—was sick and in the hospital. I tried to focus on everything at the same time. I wanted to be there for my family, for my team, for myself, for my future. I watched teammates who I knew were going to get drafted. They had that potential everyone was always talking about. I was a senior in college and already "the old guy" trying to get drafted, trying to get ahead of the younger kids on scholarships, the ones who got recruited. But I knew I was ready. I was primed to sink my teeth into that big, juicy cheeseburger. I thought it was there for the taking.

And then, just like that, it was gone. It was April 2020, right in the middle of the season, when we started hearing rumors of this virus spreading from Wuhan. They told us it would be fine. Sure, the SEC was shutting things down, but we were in the Big West conference, and everything was a go. Heck, we play outside, what was the problem? We were all getting set to head to Bakersfield for a game when we got an email: The season was cancelled.

I couldn't quite process what was happening. But I knew that everybody else was affected too. So I figured we would all just take a pause and that nobody could pass me if none of us could play. Just hang out, and we'll get it back together. People were already talking about a "Covid year" and getting an extra year of eligibility. I held on to that. My grandmother had had a severe stroke and was now

completely bedridden and living with my family and me. She became, at the very least, a way for me to focus on someone other than myself. She wasn't really verbal, so I would just try to help her eat and give her some of the same attention she gave me when I was little. Gyms were closed, so there was nothing to do but try to help out, rather than wallow in my own frustrations.

There was something that felt like old times, at least, in having all of us together under one roof. When I was little, one of the meals we used to eat all the time was a sloppy joe made from a big old can of Manwich. It was like cheap comfort in a can and a reminder of earlier days. We ate all our meals together as a family, where even food this simple could feel special.

During my first year at UC Riverside. I had just gotten my brand-new clothes after being told I made the team, and wanted to practice in them.

PREP TIME: 15 MINUTES **COOK TIME:** 50 MINUTES **MAKES** 8

To bring back some of those comfort memories, which are all jumbled together between childhood and the family bonding of Covid, I made an updated version of my family's sloppy joes, without the Manwich can. This is a Sloppy Jordan, made better than the canned stuff, because you can always improve on memories. These are made from scratch: A skillet of frothy, bubbling oil and butter is used to cook the onions, peppers, garlic, spices, tomato paste, ketchup, and mustard. Ground beef is folded in and simmered with beef bouillon, before it gets slathered onto a bun with sharp cheddar cheese and a mound of Fritos. It is pure comfort food that tastes like nostalgia, but even better than the original.

SLOPPY JORDANS WITH SHARP CHEDDAR AND FRITOS

- 1 tbsp butter
- 2 tbsp olive oil, divided
- ½ large yellow or white onion, finely chopped
- ½ red bell pepper, finely chopped
- ½ green bell pepper, finely chopped
- 2 garlic cloves, finely chopped
- Kosher or fine sea salt, to taste
- Freshly ground black pepper, to taste
- 3 tbsp tomato paste
- 2 tbsp mild American chili powder
- 1 tsp granulated garlic
- 2 tbsp ketchup
- 1 tbsp yellow mustard
- 2lb (900g) ground beef
- 2 tsp beef bouillon powder, dissolved in 1½ cups warm water
- 8 sesame seed hamburger buns
- 1lb (450g) grated sharp cheddar cheese (see note)
- 1 bag Fritos

Note: Freshly grated cheddar cheese, without binders, will melt better than pre-grated cheese.

1. Place a wide skillet or Dutch oven over medium-high heat. Add the butter and 1 tablespoon of the oil. Once the butter has melted, add the onion, bell pepper, and garlic. Season with salt and pepper and cook for about 6 minutes, stirring occasionally, until the onions are just tender.
2. Push the vegetables to one side of the pan and add the remaining tablespoon olive oil to the empty side of the pan. Add the tomato paste and stir, frying in the oil for about 30 seconds. Stir the tomato paste into the rest of the vegetables.
3. Add the chili powder and granulated garlic. Stir everything together, then add the ketchup and yellow mustard. Stir the mixture well.
4. Add the ground beef and another pinch of salt and black pepper. Stir well and cook for about 2 minutes, until most of the raw color is gone, "chopping" at the beef with a cooking spoon to break up any big pieces.
5. Stir in the beef bouillon and water. Bring to a simmer, then cover with a lid and reduce the heat to medium-low. Simmer, covered, for 20 minutes.
6. Remove the lid and bring to a strong simmer. Simmer, uncovered, for about 3 minutes more, until the sauce has a thick, stew-like consistency.
7. Taste and adjust the seasoning with more salt as needed. Cover the pot and let rest while you set up the sandwiches.
8. Toast the buns in a toaster or on a separate pan with some butter, then lay out the bottom slices and spoon a generous layer of the beef onto each. Top with the grated cheddar and a handful of Fritos, letting the chips spill off the sides and onto the plate.
9. Close the Sloppy Jordans with the bun tops and serve immediately. Leftover filling can be stored in an airtight container in the refrigerator for up to 1 week.

draft day

Even though the season was cancelled, there was still going to be an MLB draft, where the top prospects get selected by teams and usually put into their minor league and developmental teams, on the path to playing in the big leagues. "The Covid Draft," people called it. It was going to be fully remote, with none of the top prospects showing up for the live ceremony like they usually would. But in order to be eligible for the draft, you had to actually submit paperwork to the league. I didn't do that.

The thing is, I *knew* I wasn't getting drafted. I didn't have the résumé for it, and like I said, I didn't even file the paperwork. But despite all that, there was still a part of me, sitting down to watch the draft at home, that wondered to myself, "But what if they called my name anyway?" It was like experiencing the stages of grief, and maybe I was still in denial. I wanted to believe there was a chance.

I watched the names get called. I kept it to myself, but in my head, I thought, "This is about potential. It's not even about how good they are at baseball." These teams are trying to get lucky and win the lottery by finding that diamond in the rough. I still felt deep down that if I had gotten a fair shake, if I had gotten the chance to really play in that second half of the season, if I had the reps, that I could have proven myself and gotten drafted. I was at one time *so sure* I was going to pull this dream off. I thought I was going to prove everybody wrong one more time.

I sat there, watching the draft, and I was just . . . exhausted. I thought about all the hard work I put in to get to this place. I thought about all the hours, pre-Covid, when I was in the gym while everyone else was home on the couch. But in the end, there I was, and it didn't matter. I ended up at home on the couch, just like them. The rounds rolled by, and they kept calling out names, team after team, pick after pick, and my denial turned into anger. I felt like baseball beat me up. It chewed me up and spit me out.

In the aftermath, the months just rolled by. We finished classes remotely on our computers. Graduation came and went, and I don't know if I thought I was actually returning or just holding onto the idea of an extra Covid year of eligibility. I probably knew it was over, but it hadn't sunk in yet. Not until I looked at my phone and started seeing my friends on social media picking up their uniforms. I never got a call. I never got an email. It wasn't until I saw my teammates posting about the new season on Instagram that I learned they weren't having me back. My baseball career was done, and I was heartbroken. That was when it all finally set in. The part that hurt the most was that I never knew my last day playing baseball . . . was my last day playing baseball.

I had a lot of jobs after my baseball career ended. I'll detail them more later, but one of them during the months that followed was at Chipotle. I bring it up now because it was perhaps my least favorite of all the many jobs I had to take to make ends meet, all while I was growing my social media following. It provides the starkest contrast to, say, being a professional baseball player. I was a grill cook. I would grill all day, for hours on end. Opening up marinated meat, grilling, my face steaming behind a mask, dripping sweat. Open, grill, sweat, repeat. It was like working out in the gym again, but without that end-goal. It was just clocking in and clocking out, trying to do the best job I could. I'm a people pleaser after all, and I never wanted how I felt to rub off on the people around me.

Back then, I typically ate pretty light: maybe a couple of tacos to keep me on my feet without getting weighed down. Now I can't look at a Chipotle without getting upset. I like the idea of it and the food they serve, but I despise the thought of setting foot in one again. So instead, I'm taking control back, so to speak. Now I can eat my version of their burrito, without needing to see the building or even any of the packaging. I like my version better anyway.

My first game playing on a Division 1 roster in 2019. This was my first ever at bat, which was sadly a strikeout. I embarrassed myself, but at the same time, I was proud I got to say I had an at bat for a Division 1 team.

EASTON

PREP TIME: 30 MINUTES, PLUS 2-24 HOURS MARINATING TIME   COOK TIME: 1 HOUR   SERVES 4

CHIPOTLE BURRITO BOWL WITH MARINATED CHICKEN, REFRIED BEANS, BROWN RICE, AND HOMEMADE SALSA

For the Chipotle-Marinated Chicken

2 tbsp adobo sauce, from a 7oz (200g) can of chipotle in adobo
1 tbsp dried oregano
1 tbsp granulated garlic
2 tbsp neutral oil, such as vegetable or canola, divided
1 tbsp lime juice or distilled white vinegar
1 tsp kosher or fine sea salt, or more to taste
1 tsp smoked paprika
1 tsp soy sauce
1½lb (675g) boneless, skinless chicken breasts

For the Chipotle Salsa Roja

Makes about 1½ cups

8oz (225g) Roma tomatoes
2 garlic cloves, in their skins
2 chipotle peppers from a 7oz (200g) can of chipotle in adobo (or less, for a milder salsa)
Kosher or fine sea salt, to taste

For the Cilantro-Lime Brown Rice

1¼ cups long-grain brown rice
2 tbsp finely chopped cilantro
1 tbsp neutral oil, such as canola or vegetable
A squeeze of lime juice, or to taste
Kosher or fine sea salt, to taste

For the Refried Beans

1 tbsp neutral oil, such as vegetable or canola
½ cup finely chopped white onion
Kosher or fine sea salt
16oz (454g) can refried beans

Ingredient list continues on next page

CHIPOTLE-MARINATED CHICKEN

1. In a resealable container, like a Tupperware or a ziplock bag, combine the adobo, oregano, granulated garlic, 1 tablespoon of the oil, the lime juice, salt, paprika, and soy sauce. Mix until well combined.
2. Lay down some plastic wrap or open a large ziplock bag. Lay a chicken breast on the plastic wrap or place it in the bag, with some space around all sides. If using plastic wrap, lay another sheet on top. Using a heavy, flat meat mallet or a heavy-bottomed skillet, pound the breast with medium force until even and about ½ inch (1cm) thick. Repeat with the other breasts, then add them to the marinade, making sure to fully coat each. Transfer to the refrigerator to chill and marinate for at least 2 hours and up to 24.
3. When you are ready to cook the breasts, preheat a wide skillet over medium heat for 3 minutes. Add the remaining tablespoon of the oil and tilt to coat the pan. Lay the breasts down and cook for 5 to 6 minutes, until the bottoms are a nice golden brown.
4. Flip them over and repeat with the other side, cooking for 5 to 6 minutes more, until the chicken is fully cooked through (reading an internal temperature of about 150°F / 66°C).
5. Allow the chicken breasts to rest for about 2 minutes, then chop into medium cubes.

Note: To save yourself some cleanup, you can definitely grill this chicken on a gas or charcoal grill over medium-high heat in just about the same amount of time.

CHIPOTLE SALSA ROJA

1. Set a cast-iron or heavy-bottomed skillet over high heat. Place the tomatoes and unpeeled garlic cloves in the pan and char for about 10 minutes, turning as needed, until the tomatoes are softened and have black blistered skin. (Alternatively, you can place them on a baking sheet under the broiler and turn every 90 seconds until charred.)

RECIPE CONTINUES ON NEXT PAGE

For the Chipotle Burrito Bowl

1 batch Cilantro-Lime Brown Rice
1 batch Refried Beans
1 batch Chipotle-Marinated Chicken
Shredded Mexican cheese blend, or a mix of grated cheddar and Monterey Jack, to taste
Shredded iceberg lettuce, to taste
Sour cream, to taste
1 batch Chipotle Salsa Roja

2. To a blender, add the charred tomatoes. Discard the garlic skins and add the cloves to the blender, along with the chipotles and a generous pinch of salt. Blend until the salsa reaches a rough texture. Season to taste with salt.
3. Keep covered in the refrigerator for up to 1 week. Or you can leave the salsa out for several hours, covered, if you plan on eating soon after preparation.

CILANTRO-LIME BROWN RICE

1. Cook the brown rice according to package instructions.
2. While still warm, mix in the cilantro, oil, and lime juice. Mix and season with salt to taste. Keep covered to stay warm until ready to serve.

REFRIED BEANS

1. Place a medium pot over medium heat. Add the oil, onion, and a pinch of salt. Sauté for about 5 minutes, stirring occasionally, until the onion is soft and translucent.
2. Add the refried beans and stir to combine. Keep cooking for about 5 minutes, stirring occasionally, until the beans are warmed through. Depending on the brand, you may need to add a splash of water and additional salt to reach your desired consistency and seasoning. Cover to keep warm, or reheat before serving.

CHIPOTLE BURRITO BOWL

1. Line up four bowls and divide the rice equally between them.
2. Spoon the beans over top, followed by the chipotle-marinated chicken.
3. Add your desired toppings, such as cheese, lettuce, sour cream, and the Chipotle Salsa Roja, and enjoy.

the power of hearing no

I was still heartbroken after the draft. I truly was. But at the same time I felt a relief in that moment finally being over. My grandmother was still sick, and we were all just hanging around the house. It seemed like there was something missing, a sense of purpose and drive, certainly. But I felt free too. Pushing so hard for so long without any real payoff in sight carried a real level of anxiety, and any answer was better than none. People talk about the power of saying no to things, but there's an absolute power in *hearing* no too. It releases you from limbo. I'll take a "no" over a "maybe" or an "I don't know" a hundred times out of a hundred.

I thought back to all the hours and days I spent sending out emails and letters to coaches and colleges. I hear it all the time from people who want to be writers or actors, from people who are looking for work and sending out résumés, people who are just looking for the opportunity to feed themselves and their family. You pour yourself into this, crafting your cover letters for each opportunity, updating your résumé to fit a specific person or goal. You do research on the people and the companies, trying to show what it is in your life that would make you the right fit. But then after all that work, how often do you get the luxury of a response? Not even a "no," just . . . nothing. No response at all. You don't know if you failed completely or if you were just ignored. It's soul-crushing. You feel like you're screaming into a void. Did I forget to hit send? Did my application get lost? Did it get thrown in the trash? Not knowing is the hardest part. But hearing "no" is liberating. It's an answer, a real answer, and you can finally move on to what's next. I'm not going to lie and say it's as good as a "yes," but at least it makes you feel like a human being who is worthy of interaction, communication, and respect. "No" is a silver medal.

My last year playing at UC Riverside in 2019. Sadly, a few weeks after this photo was taken, I would never play the sport again because of Covid.

adidas
Riverside
LOUISVILLE

“

I was given my personality back, or at least an empty space where it was supposed to be. I had to go out and find it instead.

”

When my situation finally sank in, there was this weird feeling of empowerment that started to wash over me. My identity had been baseball for so long, and now all of a sudden it wasn't anymore. I was given my personality back, or at least an empty space where it was supposed to be. I had to go out and find it instead.

College life is a world of potential. Everything is about what you *could* do. But then you get thrown into the real world, and it's no longer about what you *will* do; it's about actually doing something.

We've all heard the stories of people who knew what they wanted to be since they were a kid, who never had a Plan B, and who achieved their dreams. Well, that wasn't me. Mine is the story of somebody who had no idea what to do when Plan A fell apart.

But speaking of saying no to things, I'll tell you something I will absolutely say no to: Lit'l Smokies. You know, those tiny smoked hot dogs that everybody in the world except for me seems to like for pigs in a blanket? The first few times I tried them, I thought I was getting seeds stuck in my teeth until I realized they were those little nubs on the end of the casing. I hated them so much. But part of growing up is finding a Plan B. Whether your baseball career is over, or you hate tiny smoked sausages, there is always a workaround and a backup option that can surprise you. In the case of Lit'l Smokies, the answer was buying good old-fashioned American hot dogs, slicing them down into bite-size pieces, and then wrapping them in crescent rolls, brushing them with garlic butter, covering them in Parmesan, baking them, and dipping them in tomato sauce. Just goes to show you that sometimes Plan B is better than Plan A anyway.

PREP TIME: 15 MINUTES COOK TIME: 15 MINUTES SERVES 8–12

BETTER PIGS IN A BLANKET WITH GARLIC BUTTER AND TOMATO DIPPING SAUCE

For the Garlic Butter

1 stick salted butter
½ tsp dried parsley
2 garlic cloves, minced
1 tsp granulated garlic
Kosher or fine sea salt, to taste

For the Better Pigs in a Blanket

8 hot dogs, such as Hebrew National
8oz (227g) can refrigerated crescent roll dough, such as Pillsbury
1 batch Garlic Butter, warmed just enough that the butter is still melted
¼ cup grated Parmesan cheese
Jarred tomato sauce or Basic Tomato Sauce (page 121), warmed, for serving, or sauce of choice, such as mustard, Cane's Sauce (page 145), or Chick-fil-A Sauce (page 127)

GARLIC BUTTER

1. In a small saucepan over medium-high heat, add the butter, parsley, minced garlic, and granulated garlic and bring to a simmer. Turn off the heat and let sit for at least 2 minutes.
2. Season with salt to taste. Leftover garlic butter can be stored, covered, in the refrigerator for up to 1 week.

BETTER PIGS IN A BLANKET

1. Preheat the oven to 375°F (190°C). Line a baking sheet with parchment paper or a Silpat baking mat for easier cleanup.
2. Cut the hot dogs cross-wise into thirds so they are about 2 inches (5cm) long each. Set aside.
3. Unfurl the crescent roll dough onto a clean work surface. Separate the dough along the perforated seams and use a knife to cut each section into three long, skinny triangles. Place a hot dog on the base of each triangle, then roll the dough up toward the tip.
4. On the prepared baking sheet, place the pigs in a blanket seam-side down, evenly spacing them out to prevent crowding.
5. Use a pastry brush or a spoon to baste the tops of each pig in a blanket with the Garlic Butter. Top with the grated Parmesan and bake for 12 to 15 minutes, until golden brown and plump. Serve warm with the tomato sauce for dipping. Leftovers can be stored in an airtight container in the refrigerator for up to 1 week.

emotional hangover

I had just turned twenty-three when my baseball career came to a screeching halt. In the short few months that followed, I was forced to grow up a bit. But the truth is, things don't operate in a straight line. Progress is up and down; it's two steps forward and one step back. Even when you tell yourself you're okay and you *feel* okay, it doesn't mean you're totally okay.

I would go about my days in full belief that I had completely accepted my fate, excited to see what was next. I would go to sleep knowing I was okay, and then I would wake up angry. I'd be tense, tired, and on the brink of tears, and somehow it would hit me as a total surprise. It would cause me to think about my baseball career again, sinking into a cycle of negative thoughts. I would tell myself it was meant to end this way, and start trying to find someone—anyone—to blame for it all being over. Was this my fault? Was it my coaches' fault? Did baseball do this to me?

I was the one who wanted to be a baseball player, I told myself. Everyone else told me not to do it. They told me I would fail, and I did. Maybe I should have listened in the first place. Eventually these feelings would subside, almost like I forgot about it. I would cool down and then suddenly, randomly, and with great ease *pick up a heavy object*, and it would jog my memory, reminding me how unnecessarily strong I was: this hulking creature who could move a refrigerator by myself if I had to. There was no reason to be this strong. But then to deal with my pent up frustration, I would go back to the gym and lift to feel better. I would squat twenty sets of 315 pounds like it was nothing. I was upset I was strong, and I would lift to feel better, perpetuating the cycle all over again. It was like an emotional hangover, recovering

During a scrimmage at San Francisco State in 2017. This was the best shape I was ever in.

from an immense letdown. I felt awful, and I would get mad at myself. I'm not a drinker, but I was sure this must be what a hangover feels like—like your body is eating you from the inside, combined with this nagging guilt that you did this to yourself.

Eventually I found comfort in things other than lifting. I would take long drives to Riverside from my parents' house in Oceanside to see friends, then return and spend time with my grandmother, who was still recovering from her stroke. I needed something to balance out my literal and philosophical anger. Communication continued to be hard for my grandmother, but the one thing she could do was laugh, and her laugh was infectious. When I made her laugh, everything became better. Sometimes she would look at me and muster the words, "My baby," and it melted my heart. It melted my anger too. When I saw her, I knew I couldn't be mad at the world, because my grandmother was in the world.

Funnily enough, these moments would make me think of oatmeal. My grandmother was the first person to give me a simple bowl of oatmeal, topped with cinnamon, apples, and maple syrup. Now it is such an associative dish for me, one that brings me so much comfort. My grandmother has since passed, and as my own passion for cooking has evolved, my oatmeal methods have too. One of my favorite ways to do it now is to make a big batch of velvety cinnamon apple butter cooked with some brown sugar and maple syrup, and then stir it into a fresh bowl of oatmeal along with a pat of butter and a sprinkle of flaky sea salt. It tastes like all the flavors she used to put in hers, but just a little bit different, a little more refined. It's a way to think of her and also to move forward. But from time to time, I do wish that she could taste it—that I could finally make it for her instead of the other way around.

“

Progress is up and down; it’s two steps forward and one step back. Even when you tell yourself you’re okay and you feel okay, it doesn’t mean you’re totally okay.

”

PREP TIME: 10 MINUTES COOK TIME: ABOUT 2 HOURS (FOR JUST THE APPLE BUTTER) SERVES 4

OATMEAL WITH HOMEMADE CINNAMON APPLE BUTTER

- 3lb (1.35kg) tart apples, such as Gala or Pink Lady, cored and chopped into ½in (1cm) pieces
- ¼ cup tightly packed light or dark brown sugar
- ¼ cup maple syrup
- 2 tsp ground cinnamon
- ¼ tsp fine sea salt, plus more to taste
- 2 cups rolled oats
- 4 tbsp salted or unsalted butter

1. In a heavy-bottomed pot with a lid, add the apples along with the brown sugar, maple syrup, cinnamon, and salt. Add 1 cup water, then stir to combine.
2. Place the pot over high heat and bring to a boil. Cover with a lid, reduce the heat to low, and keep at a steady simmer for 90 minutes, stirring occasionally.
3. Remove the pot from the heat and let cool for a few minutes. Using an immersion blender in the pot, or transferring it to the jar of a blender, blend the mixture until quite smooth.
4. Return the apple butter to the pot and place it over medium heat. Once bubbling, give it a stir, then reduce the heat to medium-low and cover partially with the lid to allow steam to escape. (The goal is to let moisture evaporate out, while limiting hot apple butter splatter.)
5. Continue cooking for about 20 minutes, stirring every few minutes, until the mixture has thickened and started to turn a caramel-brown color.
6. Cool before storing in the refrigerator, where it will keep for up to 1 week.
7. To a small pot over medium-high heat, add the oats, 4 cups water, and a touch of salt and bring to a boil. Reduce the heat to low and simmer for 5 minutes, uncovered, then turn off the heat.
8. Stir in the butter and cover the pot. Let rest for 1 to 2 minutes. Scoop into four bowls and serve dolloped with the Cinnamon Apple Butter to taste.

Note: You'll have enough Cinnamon Apple Butter for roughly 7 to 14 servings of oatmeal. But feel free to use it on anything from toast, Sweet Grits (page 32), pancakes, or waffles to pork chops.

creating out of anger

It had been four months since the draft, and I needed to channel my anger into something. I think that anger stemmed from a belief that I should have had another chance, that I was supposed to have another season of Division 1 baseball, but never got it. I thought I deserved it, even though life kept telling me that there was no such thing as what you *deserve*. I didn't understand yet that baseball isn't fair, that life isn't fair. When your time is up, your time is up.

The fate of any sports career relies on other people, some luck, and some raw talent. There are certain parts you have control over and other parts you don't. In retrospect, I was mourning the end of my career, and maybe a little stuck in the denial and anger part of it, working my way into bargaining. It was also exacerbated by the Covid of it all. Just like everyone and everything else, all my flaws were exposed by Covid and all that time spent in my own head. I wanted to get back to my life before. But I could only work out so many times. I could only talk myself up so many times. The combination of everything just completely soured my emotions. I needed to turn this anger into something other than myself.

My friend Jonah, a brilliant filmmaker, and I had been getting some random footage of me playing baseball since before the UC Riverside days, back when I was about twenty. We thought it would be for a documentary, but we never really stuck with it. Then, during Covid, I started watching documentaries, and that got me thinking that maybe this could be a way to channel my feelings. I wanted to direct my anger at the sport of baseball itself. I thought I could use our footage as a way to get back at it, to expose it for what I thought it did to me.

I started going over all the footage again, writing angry narrations about all this hard work being for nothing. The frustration was dripping from my voice. It was like I was exorcising a demon. The emotion was just something I needed to get out, to release from deep down in my stomach. It was like there were two paths I could have taken in this documentary: one of rage and one of empathy. It reminded me of—hear me out on this one—my mom's chicken enchiladas.

My mom's side of the family has some Mexican heritage in it, and she always used to ask us if we wanted red sauce or green sauce for our enchiladas. Picking one was like making a decision based entirely on your mood. I can't explain why you would pick one or the other. I don't know why people are ever "in the mood" for one food versus another. It's just a feeling. Well, for the documentary I chose anger—an emotion that is often associated with the color red. Anger can be a delicious emotion when you let it out. It can be what you need sometimes.

When my mom used to make her chicken enchiladas, she did it by creating a large amount of food all at once. We could reheat the leftovers, and they'd hold up for days. This version is inspired by her, geared toward making something delicious that isn't too much work. I'm taking a canned red enchilada sauce, cheese, and a grocery store rotisserie chicken, and leveling up the flavor with some fresh onions and garlic, dried spices, and chicken bouillon powder. It's a perfect leftovers-dish too, if you're cooking for fewer people and want some easy meals later in the week.

→

PREP TIME: 30 MINUTES COOK TIME: 30 MINUTES SERVES 4-6

EASY RED CHICKEN ENCHILADAS

1 tbsp neutral cooking oil, such as canola or avocado
1 small-to-medium white onion, diced
3 garlic cloves, finely chopped
1 tsp paprika
1 tsp granulated garlic
1 tsp dried oregano
½ tsp ground cumin
1 tsp chicken bouillon powder, or 1 bouillon cube
3 cups shredded rotisserie chicken
28oz (795g) can red enchilada sauce, divided
Kosher or fine sea salt, to taste
12 corn tortillas, white or yellow
8oz (225g) grated medium cheddar (see note), divided
8oz (225g) grated Monterey Jack (see note), divided
1 handful of cilantro leaves (optional)
Sour cream, to serve

Note: Pre-shredded cheese will absolutely work, but for the best texture, buy blocks of cheese and grate yourself. Pre-grated cheese has a coating that keeps it from clumping in the bag, but also keeps it from melting quite as well.

1. Preheat the oven to 350°F (180°C).
2. Place a medium skillet over medium heat and add the oil. Once shimmering, add the onion and garlic. Sauté, stirring occasionally, for 8 to 10 minutes, until the onion is soft and translucent.
3. Stir in the paprika, granulated garlic, oregano, and cumin, and toast for about 30 seconds. Add ½ cup water and the bouillon and bring to a simmer.
4. Add the shredded chicken and stir. Add about ½ cup of the enchilada sauce and increase the heat to medium-high. Once the sauce comes to a simmer, reduce the heat to a gentle simmer and cook for about 2 minutes. Season with salt to taste and set aside.
5. Take a spoonful of the enchilada sauce from the pan and spread it across the bottom of a 9 x 13-inch (23 x 33cm) baking dish.
6. Warm up the tortillas to make them pliable without breaking. For the easiest method, wrap them in a damp paper towel, place on a plate, and microwave on high for 45 seconds. (You can also char them one-by-one directly over the flame on your stove, or heat them in a nonstick skillet over high heat.) Keep warm in a stack, wrapped in a kitchen towel or a tortilla warmer.
7. Transfer the remaining enchilada sauce to a wide bowl and set a small plate next to it. (This plate will be to stuff and roll each tortilla without making a mess.)
8. One at a time, dip each tortilla into the enchilada sauce, coating both sides. Lay it on the plate, then fill it with a scant ¼ cup of the chicken. Sprinkle a mixture of the two cheeses over the chicken, then roll the tortilla into a tight tube and lay, seam-side down, in the baking dish. Repeat with the remaining enchiladas until you've tightly packed all twelve into the baking dish. Pour the remaining sauce over the enchiladas, and top with the remaining cheese.
9. Cover the baking dish with aluminum foil and bake for 10 minutes. Remove the foil and continue cooking for about 15 minutes more, or until the cheese and sauce are bubbling. For a crispier top, broil on high heat 1 to 2 minutes more until the cheese has browned lightly at the edges.
10. Remove from the oven and garnish with the cilantro leaves (if using). Serve hot, with the sour cream. Leftovers can be stored in an airtight container in the refrigerator for up to 1 week.

changing anger to appreciation

So . . . that angry narration I told you about? That was the first "script" I had ever tried to write in my life. I'm sitting there trying to narrate over these workout videos about how I had pushed myself so hard, I had changed my body, I had gone through so much . . .

It was incredibly long-winded, and frankly, it kind of sucked. I said to myself that if I was going to be angry, I didn't have to be so damn verbose about it. The next step was trying to write something shorter, but the funniest thing happened. When I started taking out all the excessive descriptors, some of the rage started going away too. My hate letter slowly turned into a love letter. I watched myself pushing and pushing, saw how I was excited to come back the next day and do the work again. The documentary began to take on a life of its own. This story didn't end up being about a man ruined by baseball. It was a movie about a man falling in love with it, even though the sport could never love him back. The movie was about longing. I began to feel wistful and relieved instead of betrayed. All of a sudden, it became a thing of beauty.

I had been looking at the game of baseball as a black-and-white endeavor. I thought the goal was to practice hard, get minutes, and then get drafted. But baseball was Mr. Miyagi-ing me all along. This was never really about baseball itself. This whole process, this whole ordeal, was teaching me lessons about myself, about success and failure. It was a tool, and a set of skills to better my life and my perspective.

Nowadays, I love baseball again, and the documentary helped me get there. It's funny—now I can actually watch baseball or go to games and just enjoy the experience. I see plays unfolding before they

“This was never really about baseball itself. This whole process, this whole ordeal, was teaching me lessons about myself, about success and failure.”

happen. I watch plays develop. It took me a long time to realize that baseball can just be a game. It can be a hobby that you do for *fun*, not only as a path to a career where you either succeed or fail. I don’t play much anymore, but every once in a while, it’s nice to catch a ball and throw it back. It still feels good when your bat connects with a pitch.

The older I get, the more I realize that life is about perspective. The footage we recorded all those years ago didn’t change: It was just a video of me doing squats with hundreds of pounds on my shoulders. But depending on where you are in your life when you look at it, you can view it with anger and pettiness, or you can view it as something romantic and beautiful.

PREP TIME: 7 MINUTES COOK TIME: 12 MINUTES SERVES 6–8

Perspective affects everything, even a pack of Hawaiian roll slider buns. You can look at them as a vessel for tiny burgers and get mad about having to portion out a ton of miniature beef patties. Or you can slather them in garlic butter and a tasty melty cheese, place them in a hot oven, and in a few minutes, you've got the most decadent, cheesy, pull-apart bread in the world.

PULL-APART CHEESY HAWAIIAN-ROLL GARLIC BREAD

12-pack of King's Hawaiian Sweet Rolls
1 stick salted butter, softened to room temperature
2 garlic cloves, very finely chopped
1 tsp dried parsley
1 tsp granulated garlic
Kosher or fine sea salt, to taste
8oz (225g) grated, low-moisture mozzarella
¼ cup grated Parmesan cheese

1. Preheat the oven to 400°F (200°C).
2. Place the Hawaiian rolls onto a baking dish or rimmed baking sheet, taking care to keep them all attached. Next, make long, shallow cuts through the tops of all the rolls, being careful not to cut all the way through, creating two long crevices across each row of rolls. This will allow you to stuff the cheese mixture inside the rows.
3. In a medium mixing bowl, combine the butter, chopped garlic, parsley, granulated garlic, and a pinch of salt. Stir until well combined. Taste the mixture and add more salt if needed.
4. Spread the mixture evenly across the top of the rolls. Open the slits and stuff the mozzarella inside, distributing it evenly.
5. Top the rolls with the Parmesan and bake for about 12 minutes, until the cheese is melted all the way through and the Parmesan has browned slightly.
6. Serve warm. Pull apart and enjoy! Leftovers can be stored in an airtight container in the refrigerator for up to 5 days.

learning how to self-promote

I poured myself into this documentary short. The whole thing was finished in just a week and a half. I called it *Dear Baseball.* But now I had more to do. When I was in high school, I was working hard but not always working on the right things. This time, I was ready to work more intelligently. I didn't want to just make this documentary in a vacuum and hope somebody discovered it. "The work" was finished, but the work was just beginning. The hard part about making a documentary isn't making the film itself. The hard part is getting people to watch.

I had eight hundred followers on Instagram when I began promoting this documentary, which I treated like a job. I started out by asking all eight hundred of my followers to post about my short in their stories, all the while knowing it was a burdensome ask. This was not the most efficient way to go about getting the word out. But also, did you know there's a limit to how many DMs you can send? Well, neither did I, until I sent about twenty or thirty in a row and I got a notification that I'd reached the limit.

Then I found out that there's no limit to how many people you can email, so I started looking for contact buttons for everybody I could find. Not even just famous people—I emailed *anybody*. If I found somebody who was following two thousand people, I would click on every single one of those names and send them an email. Each email was custom, but they said something along the lines of, "Hi, I'm Jordan. It's nice to meet you. I'm a former Division 1 baseball player, my grandmother recently suffered a stroke, and I have a story, in the form of a documentary short, that I'm dying to put out into the world. I think there are a lot of people out there like me, and I would be honored if you would share it."

> "The path to a brighter future was all about changing my perspective."

This went on for about two or three months, seven days a week, sending thousands of emails every single day. This was more than a full-time job—it was all-consuming. It was my new obsession. I was back in the weight room, so to speak. It was a new version, proving that my skillset was never really baseball—it was drive. I didn't want to be a baseball player anymore, I wanted to get my baseball story out there, and nothing could prevent me from doing it. To be honest, I didn't even know what I was hoping to get out of it. I just had a story, and I wanted people to hear it.

I had grown from eight hundred followers to only a thousand over two months, but the YouTube views kept ticking up. One thousand, then two thousand, three thousand. It just kept growing. Eventually, it got up to thirty thousand views, and I couldn't believe it. I was riding a high. These were real views from real people, hearing my story and passing it along to other people. I felt fulfilled in a way I hadn't in a very long time. It gave me the confidence to believe that I could make my version of what art is. I had a new sense of self. I had a new path.

As I kept discovering over and over again, the path to a brighter future was all about changing my perspective. When I hit a roadblock, in the form of DM limits, I turned my head a little and found a new way in.

It's just like when I used to work at this little fast-food joint called Angelo's Burgers. I worked there on and off from the ages of nineteen to twenty-one, almost like a summer job. There was a milkshake station, and I used to *despise* making milkshakes. It was this same motion, over and over again: Dip the scooper in cold water, put the ice cream in the blender, add milk, blend. Over and over and over. I got so bored that I started asking customers if I could add a banana to it. It may seem like nothing, but I felt like I was developing my own little personal recipe, and all of a sudden, I started enjoying making milkshakes. Customers would try it and say it was the best milkshake they had ever had. Suddenly, instead of just being a menial task, it was something that I had this tiny amount of ownership over, and this feeling of personal connection to. People would show up just to get *my* milkshake. Sometimes the smallest thing can completely change a narrative.

It is also—no matter how simple it may seem—an incredibly delicious milkshake.

TOTAL TIME: 3 MINUTES MAKES 1

COOKIES-AND-CREAM BANANA MILKSHAKE

- 3 big scoops of vanilla ice cream
- ¼ cup whole milk
- 1 banana
- ½ cup Oreo cookie crumbs

1. Put everything in a blender and blend until it's the texture of, well, a milkshake.
2. Pour the mixture into a glass. That's it. I told you it was easy. Now just relax and enjoy.

LA
Your Moving

tasting the playoffs

One day, I opened my inbox and saw a message from Uninterrupted, the media company founded by none other than LeBron James and Maverick Carter, asking if I wanted to be a part of a segment called "More than an Athlete." I couldn't believe it. I jumped at the chance. It was relatively simple: I just had to write up and then read a thirty-second letter, telling a very brief story about how I'm more than an athlete; I'm also a human being. It was a part of a series they were putting together to highlight the stories *behind* athletes, from all levels of success.

From that experience, Uninterrupted's sister company, Mile 44, wanted me to be part of a video series called "I Wanted to Do It Anyway," all about how when the odds are stacked against you, you want to keep pushing yourself, no matter what. This was my first time being a part of a real, professional film crew. All of a sudden, the crew was referring to me as "Talent." I'd never been called talented in my whole baseball career. I went from being the old washed-up guy on my college team to being the young guy with *potential*. I was reinvigorated. I felt like I was really bringing something to the table—that my brain was the material instead of my body.

To film my part, the producers had me get back on the baseball field. They wanted footage of me on the field, throwing and hitting. It had been a year and half since I had last set foot on a baseball field, and I was so damn rusty and kind of struggling out there. And then, right at the end of the reel, I finally connected and knocked the ball out of the field. You can hear the pure exasperation and happiness, encapsulated in a relief-filled "Woo!" flying out of my mouth when it happened. It was baseball as entertainment instead of competition.

With my brother and my friend Fred in 2017. We were helping move our friend Jonah's mom across town. Just a great time and a good break from the constant grind of baseball.

Now, mind you, this wasn't an open lane into a new career or anything. Nobody was knocking down my door, shoving job offers in my face. I couldn't even put words to it at the time, but I saw a spark of an idea, that maybe there was a career path for me in storytelling, in being in front of the camera, and in providing entertainment. I felt like the young upstart who makes the playoffs and gets knocked out by the juggernaut at top speed. But I tasted possibility and I wanted more. I didn't know if I was any good at it, but I wanted to work really hard to find out.

Much further along in my social-media career, in 2024, I had a similar experience of discovering a new avenue opening up for me. There was a viral recipe for brown butter cookie dough croissants. I had been recreating viral food on my accounts already, but when I made this one—a store-bought croissant that you then bake chocolate-chip cookie dough inside and on top of—it was the first time that my version looked anything like the ones I had seen online. I was so excited and happy, and then I tasted it, this flakiness and sweet, buttery crunch, melding together in one amazing pastry, and my joy skyrocketed. The recipe, and the video, were a hit. It was like this new opportunity presented itself to me, and opened my eyes to my abilities and a whole new world of options. This level of success on a recipe recreation was something I never expected, and once I experienced it, I couldn't wait to keep going after it.

Here is my version of that same viral recipe, with homemade brown butter (because brown butter makes everything taste better). This will make you as excited as I was, even with the most boring grocery-store croissants.

“

I tasted possibility and I wanted more. I didn’t know if I was any good at it, but I wanted to work really hard to find out.

”

PREP TIME: 5 MINUTES COOK TIME: 23 MINUTES MAKES 15

BROWN-BUTTER CHOCOLATE-CHIP COOKIE CROISSANT

- 2 sticks unsalted butter, softened to room temperature
- 1½ cups tightly packed light or dark brown sugar
- ½ cup granulated white sugar
- 2 eggs, at room temperature
- 2 tsp vanilla extract
- 3¼ cups all-purpose flour
- 1¼ tsp baking powder
- 1 tsp fine sea salt
- 1¼ cups semisweet chocolate chips
- 15 store-bought croissants

1. To a medium saucepan over medium heat, add the butter and cook for about 5 minutes, stirring frequently with a whisk or wooden spoon, until browned and nutty in aroma. Turn off the heat and allow the brown butter to cool to room temperature.
2. To a large mixing bowl, add the brown sugar and granulated sugar. Pour in the brown butter and stir to combine. Add the eggs and vanilla extract and stir to combine. Add in the flour, baking powder, and salt and mix thoroughly. Finally, fold in the chocolate chips.
3. Preheat the oven to 350°F (180°C). Line a rimmed baking sheet with parchment paper.
4. Cut open the croissants like you're going to make a sandwich on a hinged roll, cutting almost all the way through. Lay onto the prepared baking sheet and spoon a generous tablespoon of the dough mixture inside each croissant, spreading into an even layer as best as you can.
5. Bake for 5 minutes, to parcook the inside, then remove from the oven.
6. Spread the remaining cookie dough across the tops of all the croissants, trying your best to divide the mixture evenly among them.
7. Return the baking sheet to the oven and bake for about 12 minutes more, until the cookie tops are browned and just cooked through.
8. Allow to cool slightly and then enjoy. Leftovers can be stored in an airtight container for up to 5 days.

finding my voice

Social media in general had never been a big factor for me when I was in high school and college, since I was so singularly focused on baseball. But after my stint with Mile 44, I started watching TikTok a lot more and was so impressed by how talented everyone was. I was beginning to think that content creation was a path I could go down and enjoy. It was like I was a kid in school all over again; everybody could sing or draw or paint except for me. I knew how to lift heavy things and hit balls. What was I going to bring to the table? I felt like a zero-tool baseball player again. "What am I good at?" I asked myself. I was stumped.

But life is just a series of challenges, and this was another one. The lesson for me was that I had to get outside my bubble and try. If I failed, I failed, but I had to try. Plus, I realized that if failure was a video getting no views, then I had nothing to be embarrassed about because nobody would see it. I was okay with that.

Funnily enough, I kept the same social media handle I had when I first set up an account as a teenager: "Jordan the Stallion." It was just something to have, before I had any clue I would do it for a living. Megan Thee Stallion was popular, and I was squatting a lot back then and had strong legs, so I just put the username in and never thought about it. Cut to years later, and it's a funny social-media name that people still ask me about.

I started out by just watching my brother, who would film himself standing in the mirror, talking about current events, or silly things like what your astrological sign means about your personality. He would literally just stand there and give his opinion on what was happening in the world. He was quick-witted, funny, a little sarcastic, and a little serious. He was himself.

"Creating social-media content became like a comfort food for me."

I did my version of copying him, just standing in the mirror and filming myself. But my first posts on TikTok were lip-synch videos. I would take the audio from a scene of a movie I liked—I can't even remember which ones—and act it out while lip-synching over them. I had fun, and it was the start of my new journey. I would give it a try and not think too much about it, then get back on the horse and try it again. Some people look at influencer and social-media success, whether that's views or money or brand deals, and they think it's ridiculous. But I never did. I just saw these videos as a way to express myself and have total control in what I said and what I put out into the world. I looked at these posts as an opportunity to let go of any vanity or insecurity, to not think about how I looked and just be free. Creating social-media content became like a comfort food for me. I was working on feeling better about myself. I wanted to feel like something other than a failed baseball player, and this was my chance to do that, to feel comfortable in my own skin as this new me.

PREP TIME: **5 MINUTES** COOK TIME: **1 HOUR** SERVES **2**

When it comes to being comforted, one of my all-time favorite ways is with grilled cheese and tomato soup. If it's a cold, rainy day, or if I'm feeling sick, this combination is one of my absolute go-to dishes to warm my soul and feel a little bit better. Since this is my cookbook, I wanted to level it up and add some luxury to it. Enter: the lobster. This recipe will not just make you a nice meal; it will also teach you how to poach a perfect lobster tail, then chop it up, season it beautifully, and lay it into a classic grilled cheese, all served alongside a deeply comforting homemade tomato soup.

LOBSTER GRILLED CHEESE AND TOMATO SOUP

2 tbsp kosher or fine sea salt, plus more to taste
Peels and juice from one lemon (see note)
6 garlic cloves, 4 peeled and smashed with the side of a knife, 2 finely chopped, divided
6oz (175g) raw or defrosted small lobster tails (about 2)
3 tbsp mayo
2 tbsp minced chives
2 tbsp finely chopped parsley leaves
1 tsp granulated garlic
½ tsp paprika
Freshly ground black pepper, to taste
1 tbsp room-temperature butter, plus more for spreading
1 tbsp olive oil
¼ cup diced yellow onion
1 tbsp tomato paste
28oz (794g) can whole, peeled tomatoes
3 tbsp cold butter, cubed
¼ cup heavy cream
4 slices of sourdough sandwich bread
3 slices of American cheese

1. In a medium pot, place 4 cups water, the salt, lemon peels, and the four peeled and smashed garlic cloves and bring to a simmer, stirring until the salt is dissolved.
2. Reduce the heat to low. Once the water stops bubbling, add the lobster tails. Gently poach just below a simmer for about 3 minutes, or until the lobsters are just barely cooked through but not rubbery, ideally reading an internal temperature of around 140°F (60°C). Meanwhile, prepare a large bowl with an ice bath.
3. Lift the lobster from the water and plunge into the ice bath to stop it from cooking. Chill for about 4 minutes.
4. Remove the lobster meat from the tails. The easiest way is to use kitchen scissors to cut lengthwise down the center of the softer inner shell. Repeat with the other, harder side, then peel the shell back and remove the lobster tail. Cut the tail meat into roughly ½-inch (1cm) chunks.
5. In a small mixing bowl, combine the mayo, chives, parsley, lemon juice, granulated garlic, and paprika and season with black pepper to taste. Stir to combine and season with salt to taste. Gently fold in the lobster meat, then set the lobster salad aside in the fridge to chill.
6. In a medium pot with a lid over medium heat, add the room-temperature butter and the olive oil. Once the butter has melted, add the onion, the finely chopped garlic, and a pinch of salt. Sauté for about 8 minutes, stirring occasionally, until the onions are translucent and tender.
7. Add the tomato paste and increase the heat to medium-high. Stir and toast for 45 seconds, then add the canned tomatoes. Use a wooden spoon to break up the whole tomatoes a little, then add a pinch of salt, and bring everything to a strong simmer, stirring occasionally. Cover with a lid, reduce the heat to low, and gently simmer for 30 minutes, just to take the raw flavor off the tomatoes.

RECIPE CONTINUES ON NEXT PAGE

8. Using either an immersion blender in the pot, or transferring the soup to a blender (if using a blender, make sure to allow the soup to cool down a bit first, for safety), blend for 10 seconds, then with the blender still running, add the cold butter cubes and cream, blending until velvety and creamy. Return to the pot if using a blender, and rewarm before serving.
9. Season with salt and freshly ground black pepper to taste and reduce the heat to low.
10. Meanwhile, place a cast-iron or nonstick skillet over medium heat and allow it to preheat for at least 2 minutes. Lay out two slices of the bread and spoon half the lobster salad onto each. Top with the cheese, ripping one of the slices in half to fit across the gaps of both the wider sourdough slices. Close the sandwiches with the remaining slices of bread.
11. Spread some room-temperature butter on the top of both sandwiches, then lay them butter-side down into the skillet. Toast for 2 to 3 minutes, until the first side is golden brown. Butter the tops of the bread, then carefully flip the sandwiches and grill the other side for another 2 to 3 minutes.
12. Cut the sandwiches in half diagonally and serve with the warm tomato soup. Leftover soup can be stored in an airtight container in the refrigerator for up to 1 week.

Note: Peel your lemon before juicing for the lobster salad.

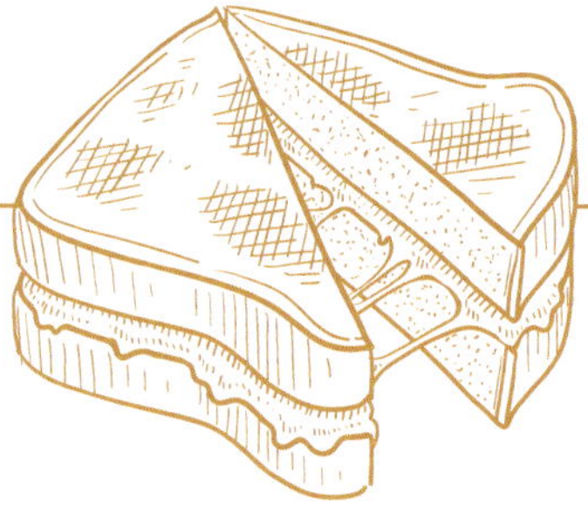

“

I wanted to feel like something other than a failed baseball player, and this was my chance to do that, to feel comfortable in my own skin as this new me.

”

the least talented person in my family

Everybody in my family has amazing talent. My dad is a great singer and musician, and he's charismatic and an amazing storyteller. My mom can draw and make things out of essentially nothing, whether it's turning paper into origami or kitchen scraps into tacos. My dad's mom, Valerie, is a tremendous cook. My brother can draw, sing, act, and make music.

I remember when I was growing up that my brother was going to be in a talent show, and I absolutely refused to take part. *It's a talent show*, I thought, *and I don't have a talent.* I remember when he got on stage and played his guitar and sang, and everyone loved it. The audience clapped and howled. He looked like a superhero. I'm gonna be honest: I don't remember what he sang, because I think my jealousy was blocking my ears. Meanwhile, I'd seen my dad perform for crowds at a local amphitheater at the state fair. It was beautiful. I admired his abilities so much.

Recently, though, just back in July 2025, I went to a Broadway show in New York for the very first time. I can't even remember what the musical was, but there was this woman who took the stage and started singing, and her voice was so powerful that it forced chills out of my body. It was magnetic and electric all at once. Nobody had phones out; they were just looking on with absolute awe. "That is pure talent," I thought. That was what very few people were blessed with. But talent like that . . . it needs an audience to exist; otherwise you may as well just perform alone in the shower. Talent doesn't matter if you don't have somebody to share it with. There are people who make music and people who listen to music. I listen.

"Talent doesn't matter if you don't have somebody to share it with."

Here's me: I am less naturally talented at singing, dancing, and performing than every other person in my family. If you were placing bets on which one of us would become an entertainer, my odds would have been the absolute worst. Nobody would have bet on me, including myself. But that just meant I had an uphill battle ahead of me.

Think of manicotti, one of the great Italian dishes. It is quite literally an empty shell that needs to be filled with something else. Every shell can look the same, but until you get into it, you don't know what's in there. It could be everything you love inside . . . or it could be your least favorite filling in the world.

I am like this recipe for manicotti: an empty shell that requires some salt, creativity, and hidden work to become the best version of itself. Maybe it's not for everybody, but I love what's on the inside, and I hope you do too.

PREP TIME: 10 MINUTES COOK TIME: 1 HOUR 30 MINUTES SERVES 6–8

This is my favorite manicotti: stuffed with ground beef, mozzarella, spinach, and ricotta, blanketed with a homemade tomato sauce, and roasted in the oven to bubbly perfection. It's simple and nuanced all at once. It is also a great make-ahead dish that you can use to feed a crowd, or make as meal prep and chow down on for the entire week. This is a hit. Just wait until you get in there and find out for yourself.

BEEF AND RICOTTA MANICOTTI

For the Basic Tomato Sauce

2 tbsp olive oil
8 garlic cloves, finely chopped
Kosher or fine sea salt, to taste
1 tsp dried oregano
Pinch of crushed red pepper
2 tbsp tomato paste
Two 28oz (794g) cans of whole, peeled tomatoes
2 sprigs fresh basil, or 2 tsp dried basil leaves

For the Manicotti

2 tbsp olive oil
½ large yellow onion, diced
5 garlic cloves, finely chopped
Kosher or fine sea salt, to taste
Freshly ground black pepper, to taste
5oz (142g) container of baby spinach
1lb (450g) ground beef
1 tsp dried oregano leaves
1lb (450g) manicotti pasta
1lb (450g) whole milk ricotta, ideally the smooth American style
1lb (450g) grated low-moisture mozzarella
½ cup finely grated Parmesan, plus more for topping
1 batch Basic Tomato Sauce

BASIC TOMATO SAUCE

1. In a medium pot over medium heat, add the olive oil.
2. Once it is shimmering, add the garlic and a pinch of salt. Sauté for about 3 minutes, stirring occasionally, until the garlic is just starting to brown at the edges.
3. Add the oregano and crushed red pepper and toast for 10 seconds, then add the tomato paste. Increase the heat to medium-high and stir the tomato paste, letting it toast for 30 seconds.
4. Crush the tomatoes by pulsing in a food processor or with an immersion blender to a rustic, chunky texture, then add the tomatoes and their juices as well as another pinch of salt to the pot. Bring to a strong simmer, then add the basil and stir.
5. Reduce the heat to low and gently simmer, covered, for 20 minutes. Turn off the heat and season with salt to taste.

MANICOTTI

1. Set a large pot of well-salted water over high heat and bring to a boil.
2. Preheat the oven to 400°F (200°C).
3. Meanwhile, in a wide skillet over medium-high heat, add the olive oil. When it is shimmering, add the onion, garlic, a pinch of salt, and a few twists of black pepper. Cook for about 5 minutes, stirring frequently, until the onion has begun to soften and brown a little at the edges.
4. Add the spinach and cook until the greens are wilted. Add the beef and oregano and season with salt and pepper to taste. Cook for about 5 minutes more, stirring frequently, until mostly browned.
5. If necessary, pour off and discard as much of the liquid as you can without too much trouble. Transfer the beef mixture to a large mixing bowl and set aside to cool for about 5 minutes.
6. Meanwhile, cook the pasta according to package instructions, removing them 1 minute before is recommended for an al dente texture (it will keep cooking in the oven). Drain the pasta and rinse under cold water.

RECIPE CONTINUES ON NEXT PAGE

7. To the bowl with the beef, add the ricotta, as well as ¾ of the mozzarella and all of the Parmesan. Mix thoroughly, then season with salt to taste.
8. Into a large casserole dish (or two small baking dishes), ladle enough of the tomato sauce to lightly coat the bottom. Using your hands, stuff the pasta with the beef mixture. Pack each one snugly into the casserole dish until completely filled (you might have a few extra manicotti noodles left over).
9. Ladle the rest of the sauce over the manicotti, or as much as you can fit without overflowing, letting the sauce flow into the gaps. Top with the remaining mozzarella and more grated Parmesan.
10. Bake for 30 to 35 minutes, until the sauce is bubbling and the cheese is browned. Let rest for 5 minutes before serving. Leftovers can be stored in an airtight container in the refrigerator for up to 5 days.

With my first-ever car in 2017. I started driving and was able to feel a little more independent. I was still trying to achieve my baseball dream. Little did I know, this car would also be where I lived for a while.

“

I am like this recipe for manicotti: an empty shell that requires some salt, creativity, and hidden work to become the best version of itself.

”

telling stories in the mirror

If I'm well known for anything, it's probably for standing in a bathroom and talking in front of a mirror. Posting these videos obviously wasn't necessarily a plan I had, and I definitely never imagined it would turn into a *career.* It was just a situation where I knew I wanted to give social media a shot, but I didn't know how to start. Even though I was copying my brother's method of filming myself in front of the mirror, when I look back, it shouldn't really be a surprise that I ended up finding comfort in that most private of rooms.

I've always talked to myself, and I would frequently do that in the bathroom, which was always a safe space for me. In my bathroom or in my car, I could be myself with no judgment. I could talk through my feelings, as funny as that may sound. But there's safety and privacy in an enclosed space like that. It's a chance to relax and not have to present as anything other than how I truly feel in a moment.

When I first started making these videos, I was trying to figure out where to look. I was just talking to myself and hadn't quite figured out yet that I was supposed to be speaking to the audience. Yet in the beginning, when I was still coming back from being a guy whose personality was tied to being a baseball player, I found peace by talking in the mirror, trying to find my personality again. I didn't have a lot of friends to talk to and was hoping that somebody out there would find what I was saying relatable, and I was in a constant battle of trying not to feel silly while doing it. Mind you, this was not profound or deep stuff. I was literally saying things like, "Do you like the Olive Garden? I found a recipe for breadsticks online."

The hardest part for me at the beginning was confronting my physical appearance, whether I looked "good enough." I thought

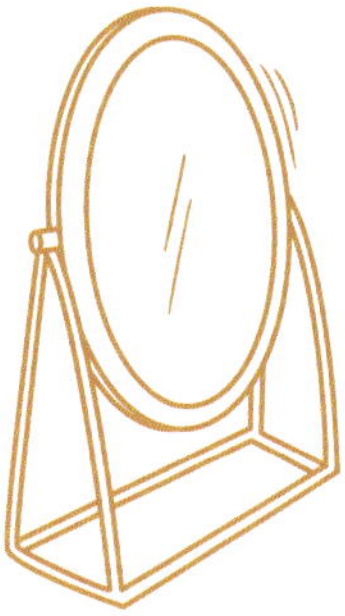

social-media influencers were supposed to be camera ready and conventionally attractive, which was something I never saw in myself. My solution was to start making videos right when I woke up, so my hair was undone, with crust still in my eyes, so I could be totally raw and bypass the feeling that I needed to look "good." If I looked bad, or at least raw, I wouldn't have to worry about being attractive.

To my surprise, people were connecting. That basic feeling of somebody commenting at all made me feel like a person who was being seen, even if they literally just commented, "I like those breadsticks too. I'll try to make them. Thanks." I felt like this totally insecure, inward-facing person who nobody would ever have expected to be an internet personality or an influencer. I was a guy who worked out in the dark, who felt like I had no skills. But my introspection turned outward was the unlikely combination that gradually turned into success.

Speaking of unlikely combinations that turn out amazing: What about multigrain bread and Chick-fil-A sauce? For this recipe, I'm updating the hotel-pool menu classic that is a club sandwich, filling it with grilled chicken and crispy bacon, but laying it onto bran-rich multigrain bread and dipping it into my Chick-fil-A sauce dupe. It's all the flavor of Chick-fil-A, without having to mess around with deep-frying chicken. Obviously, you can cheat this with cold cuts, but I want to teach you how to butterfly and grill a seasoned chicken breast, then build the club sandwich of my dreams. I love it with this dump-and-stir dipping sauce served on the side instead of on the sandwich, to keep it cleaner and easier to eat. I really don't like coleslaw dressing, but for whatever reason, it is an important ingredient in Chick-fil-A sauce. Honestly, you can just close your eyes and pick one at random for this recipe.

CHICKEN BACON CLUB WITH CHICK-FIL-A DIPPING SAUCE

For the Chick-fil-A Sauce

Makes a generous ¾ cup

½ cup coleslaw dressing

¼ cup barbecue sauce of choice

1½ tbsp yellow mustard

1 tsp lemon juice

1 tsp honey

For the Chicken Bacon Club

1 small boneless, skinless chicken breast (about 6oz / 175g)

Kosher or fine sea salt

Freshly ground black pepper

½ tsp granulated garlic

½ tsp Italian seasoning or dried oregano

1 tbsp olive oil or neutral oil, such as canola or vegetable

3 slices of multigrain bread

Salted butter

1–2 slices of sharp cheddar

3 slices of cooked, crispy bacon

3 leaves of crisp iceberg lettuce

1 batch Chick-fil-A Sauce

CHICK-FIL-A SAUCE

1. In a small mixing bowl, combine the coleslaw dressing, barbecue sauce, mustard, lemon juice, and honey and whisk until fully combined.
2. Store in a tightly sealed container in the refrigerator for up to 1 week.

CHICKEN BACON CLUB

1. Butterfly your chicken breast: Lay it flat on the cutting board. Place your nondominant palm on top of the breast to steady it while using your knife to slice it in half horizontally and lengthwise through the breast. Continue slicing until you are about 1 inch (2.5cm) from the back, then open it like a book, slicing the "spine" in any places necessary to help flatten it to an even thickness. Pat dry with paper towels, then season it on all sides with salt, freshly ground black pepper, granulated garlic, and Italian seasoning.
2. Place a skillet over medium-high heat. Allow it to preheat for about 2 minutes, then add the oil. Once it is shimmering, add the chicken breast. Use a spatula to gently press down to create more contact points with the pan. Cook for about 4 minutes, until the bottom is golden brown. Flip over and cook for about 3 minutes more, until the chicken breast is just cooked through (the internal temperature in the thickest part should reach at least 150°F / 66°C). Remove from the pan and let rest for 2 minutes.
3. Toast the slices of bread. Meanwhile, cut the chicken breast on a diagonal bias to make thin, wide slices.
4. Butter one side of one piece of toast. Begin layering the sandwich, starting with the sliced chicken breast, followed by the cheddar. Butter another slice of bread and lay it butter-side down on top of the cheddar. Butter the top side of that slice, then lay the bacon down. Top with the stack of iceberg, then butter the last slice of bread and lay that on top. Imagine cutting the sandwich into four quarters, then stick toothpicks in the centers of those quarters, pressing down with your palm as you insert them. Cut the sandwich into quarters, and serve with the Chick-fil-A Sauce on the side.

transferring my competitiveness to social media

I was about six months into my social media foray, still posting only on TikTok, and being very lax about it. It was a side project I didn't think about as a real career path. I was just talking about my day and posting maybe one or two videos a week. I had grown to about eighty thousand followers in that time, and the videos were starting to resonate a little—maybe thirty thousand views, two thousand likes, and two hundred comments on most. Then sometimes a video would get, like, a hundred thousand views, which would make me happy. If a video went viral, I would think, "Cool!" and then go back to one of the two jobs I always seemed to have at a time. (More on this later, but it was a lot of fast-food jobs, like Krispy Kreme, and other odd jobs back then). TikTok was just a fun little thing I was doing in my spare time. Then one day, I was sitting with my friend Kianna, someone whose opinion means the world to me. We were sitting in the car, and she just turned to me and said, "You're being very lazy." I was taken aback. I had been called a lot of things in my life, but lazy was never one of them.

"There are people on this earth who could really use the good fortune that you have right now, and you're not taking advantage of this incredible opportunity," she said. "You're not taking it seriously." I got defensive. What did she know about me, and everything I was going through? I was the obsessive guy, right? And there I was, just enjoying something as a hobby and not obsessing over it. But I gave it a few days and sat on what she said, and realized she was right. That was when I began to think about this whole social-media thing differently.

I started looking around at other people with a similar number of followers. I started looking analytically at what they were doing. How often were they posting? How fast were they growing their following?

My old baseball brain kicked in again. I was getting competitive: I was Superman, and I turned them into my Lex Luthor. I had to beat them. I was getting more precise in what I wanted to post, making my opinions shorter, faster, funnier, and more concise. I also upped the frequency, always wanting to post more than them. As soon as I surpassed them and reached another level of followers, I would find another round of people to compete with and try to surpass them too. Funnily enough, I still wasn't posting any cooking; it was more commentary and reactions. But my account kept growing and growing, and eventually I stopped competing with other people and started competing with myself. How can I make the videos better, cleaner, funnier? If I got one viral video in a day, could I make it two? If I make it two in a day, could I make it three? It was about improving myself. How do I sustain this growth and move forward? I had taken my friend's words to heart. I was pushing myself and seeing where it would take me.

Creating food content is messy, delicious, and ridiculously fun.

The truth is, I wasn't eating the healthiest food at that moment in my life. I was surviving on fast food from work, and maybe some basic stuff from a bag out of the freezer, chucked into an air fryer. But now, if I want to work hard, have pleasure, and eat something nutritious, I will make this salad. This is a fantastic meal that keeps the machinery operating at maximum efficiency. It is also the easiest, fastest Caesar dressing you'll ever make.

PREP TIME: 20 MINUTES COOK TIME: 25 MINUTES SERVES 2 AS A LARGE MEAL, OR 3-4 FOR A SLIGHTLY MORE MODEST ONE

SEARED SALMON CAESAR WITH PARMESAN CROUTONS

For the Easy Caesar Dressing

- ½ cup finely grated Parmesan cheese
- ¼ cup mayo
- 2 tbsp freshly squeezed lemon juice
- 2 tbsp olive oil
- 2 garlic cloves, grated
- ½ tsp Worcestershire sauce
- ½ tsp Dijon mustard
- Kosher or fine sea salt, to taste
- Freshly ground black pepper

For the Parmesan Croutons

- ¼ cup olive oil
- 4 slices of sourdough bread, cubed
- 1 tsp granulated garlic
- ½ tsp smoked or plain paprika
- Kosher or fine sea salt, to taste
- Freshly ground black pepper
- 1 cup finely grated Parmesan cheese, divided

For the Seared Salmon

- 4 heads of romaine lettuce
- Two 4–6oz (115–175g) skin-on salmon fillets
- Olive oil
- Kosher or fine sea salt, to taste
- Freshly ground black pepper
- 1 tsp dried oregano
- 1 batch Easy Caesar Dressing
- 1 batch Parmesan Croutons
- Grated Parmesan cheese, to garnish
- Lemon wedges, to serve

EASY CAESAR DRESSING

1. In a medium mixing bowl, combine the Parmesan, mayo, lemon juice, olive oil, garlic, Worcestershire sauce, mustard, a pinch of salt, and several twists of freshly ground black pepper. Whisk until combined, taste for seasoning and adjust as needed, and set aside.
2. The dressing will keep for 2 days, covered, in the refrigerator but is best enjoyed the same day.

PARMESAN CROUTONS

1. Preheat the oven to 375°F (190°C).
2. To a large mixing bowl, add the olive oil and bread and toss until well combined. Sprinkle in the granulated garlic, paprika, a pinch of salt, and a few twists of freshly ground black pepper. Toss to combine, then add half the Parmesan and toss again.
3. On a baking sheet, spread the croutons into a single layer. Bake for about 15 minutes, rotating the sheet halfway through, until they are browned and crispy. Once they are finished, return them to the mixing bowl, add the remaining cheese, and toss. Taste for salt and season with more, if desired.

SEARED SALMON

1. Preheat the oven to 400°F (200°C).
2. Cut the lettuce into bite-size pieces and transfer them to a large mixing bowl.
3. Place an oven-safe skillet on the stove over high heat.
4. Pat the salmon fillets dry with paper towels. Coat both lightly with oil and season with salt and pepper on all sides. Sprinkle the oregano on the flesh side of the fish, then lay them skin-side down into the pan.
5. Reduce the heat to medium and cook for about 30 seconds. Use your fingers or a spatula to press down gently on the fillets to create more contact with the pan. Keep cooking for about 3 minutes, or until the skin is golden brown and crispy.
6. Transfer the pan to the oven and continue cooking until the fillets are cooked to your liking. I prefer an internal temperature of about 140°F (60°C), where it is just barely cooked and tender, which takes about 2 minutes more (or slightly longer if the salmon fillets are especially thick). Remove the pan from the oven.
7. To the bowl with the lettuce, add the dressing and half the croutons and mix thoroughly. Season with salt to taste, then divide the salad between two big bowls.
8. Top each portion with one salmon fillet, skin-side up. Garnish with the Parmesan, freshly ground black pepper, and additional croutons. Serve immediately with a lemon wedge.

going viral does not mean making money

I was twenty-five years old, holding down two full-time jobs and going viral often. I would post a video that would get over a million views and a hundred thousand likes, then go to work on a construction site, post another video after work, and go to my job at a movie theater. I was an influencer people would consider successful, but I certainly still needed to make money from both jobs. I was now posting on TikTok, YouTube, Instagram, Facebook, and Snapchat, mostly cross-posting the same videos on all platforms.

But let me set the stage. It was 2022, and social media was a mixed bag. TikTok videos were about everything from current events and pop culture to singing videos, dancing trends, and makeup tutorials. It was all out there. Meanwhile, YouTube was trying to drive people away from TikTok (the "cool" platform) by offering stronger monetization—the catch-all term for earning money from your content, based on view counts. But with that monetization came rules. If their algorithms or mandates, for whatever reason, deemed your video a copyright violation or flagged it as violence, harassment, or a safety concern, they would deactivate monetization, and you would not be able to receive ad revenue for that video. I never turned on the monetization, so I'm not sure how much money I was missing out on, but I was happier that way. They had these lengthy, impenetrable terms and conditions, and I certainly wasn't reading those. It almost felt random at times. Sometimes I would cut an apple with a knife, and they would say it was a safety violation.

But money, truthfully, was not my goal. I just wanted to make videos, tell stories, and keep growing. Sometimes the videos would make money and sometimes they wouldn't, but it was never anywhere close enough to stop working two jobs. I made my videos my way,

After the scrimmage in San Francisco in 2017, we went to the Golden Gate Bridge. We had run out of money and were worried we weren't gonna get back home.

all while working real jobs straight through from five o'clock in the morning to ten o'clock at night, six days a week.

My construction job was incredibly difficult, but probably not in the way one expects. I wasn't swinging a hammer. Instead, it was my job to keep an eye on freelance workers and fire people who were milking the clock. I was, essentially, a snitch—just a young kid who was being forced to fire adults with families and responsibilities. Sometimes they weren't even slacking off, but the foreman would send me to do the dirty work nobody wanted to do, just to cut their labor costs. It was awful and stressful, and it went against my morals. I was always someone who believed in working harder than everyone else, proving my worth, and being useful and available. But with that job, I learned that sometimes you end up just teaching people how to treat you. I was the person who would do more and work harder for less money, and as a result, people took advantage of me. I was the person they wrote off, the guy who would never complain, the guy they wouldn't give even a one dollar raise to.

Not every job is an opportunity for growth. Not all are on a corporate ladder. In this case, the ladder was just coated with grease. I hated that job. I couldn't wait to leave. It was suffering in exchange for money.

But the movie theater job? That was all about the perks: free movie tickets. On days off, I would watch as many movies as I could, sometimes three in one day. It was an escape from the other job I hated so much. So there I was, doing something I loved that paid no money; doing something I hated for *some* money; and doing a third thing just for the escape of going to the movies. It was the mix of all these unorthodox jobs coming together that built me up into who I was trying to become. It was a ton of work, and I was pushing so hard, so desperate to find satisfaction in my day-to-day. It was unsustainable, and a breaking point was on the horizon.

"

I was pushing so hard, so desperate to find satisfaction in my day-to-day. It was unsustainable, and a breaking point was on the horizon.

"

PREP TIME: **5 MINUTES** COOK TIME: **15 MINUTES** SERVES **4**

Did you know that you don't have to work at a movie theater, or even go to one, to eat popcorn? In fact, if you make it yourself, you can make it exactly how you want it. The better version is always at your fingertips if you learn how to do it yourself. That's how I ended up with my favorite popcorn in the world: a sweet, fatty, salty, crunchy popcorn, thanks to a little brown sugar and bacon grease.

BROWN SUGAR–BACON GREASE POPCORN

1 tsp high-heat oil, like canola, vegetable, or avocado
4 slices of thick-cut bacon, diced
½ cup popcorn kernels
1 tbsp light or dark brown sugar
Fine sea salt, to taste

1. Place a medium skillet over medium heat. Add the oil, and once it is shimmering, add the diced bacon and cook for about 10 minutes, stirring occasionally, until the bacon is crispy and the fat is rendered.
2. Pour the contents through a strainer into a heavy-bottomed pot with a lid, like a Dutch oven. Set the strained bacon aside on a paper towel–lined plate.
3. Place the pot with the bacon fat over medium-low heat and add two popcorn kernels. Cover the pot and allow them to cook until they pop (this is how you will know the fat is ready).
4. Add the remaining popcorn kernels and cover the pot, leaving the lid ever so slightly ajar to allow steam to escape but not the popped popcorn. Increase the heat to medium and continue cooking, shaking the pan frequently. As you continue to shake the pot, listen closely until you don't hear any popping for 3 to 5 seconds, usually 3 to 4 minutes total cooking time. Once the popping has subsided, turn off the heat.
5. Remove the lid and transfer the popcorn to a large mixing bowl. Add the brown sugar, reserved bacon, and a pinch of salt. Toss to combine well, crumbling the bacon into pea-sized pieces. Season with more salt to taste. Enjoy warm. Leftovers can be stored in an airtight container for up to 5 days.

your life is what you do every day

I ended up leaving both those jobs. Construction was crushing my heart, and the movie theater eventually reduced the number of free movie tickets for employees. Stepping away from the stress and anxiety of those jobs crystalized something for me and made me realize that the life I wanted was not the life that I had. I wanted to change how I viewed work. I didn't want to live a life in which I had to beg a boss for a promotion or a few extra bucks per hour. I wanted to live my life to enjoy what I was doing, every single day. I love routine. I wanted my version of happy monotony, or at least something to look forward to.

It made me think back to my teens and early twenties, when I worked summers at that local burger place called Angelo's. It was the kind of place that had everything you could think of, besides spaghetti. I was happy there. They had wanted to make me the manager, but I'd avoided it like the plague. I didn't want to turn it into something I hated just for a little more money. Instead, I chose my menial job with low expectations and free food. I hooked up my friends, and I enjoyed the benefits of a low-stress job.

But more than anything? I loved the morning shift, my oasis. I would clock in at 6 a.m., turn on ESPN, and start setting up the restaurant. I took my "lunch break" as early as I possibly could and would eat some breakfast with the TV on and watch the sunrise over the lagoon. That was more precious to me than money could ever be. If I had that morning routine and a paycheck every two weeks, I was happy.

I kept this idea in my head when I left the construction and movie jobs, and instead found pleasure from working the evening shift at Krispy Kreme. I had a cool night manager, and we listened to music and gave out the end-of-the-night donuts before they were thrown away. My manager played this same playlist of eighties and nineties music every night, and I knew that once "Return of the Mack" came on, we had an hour left of the shift and the night was about to get fun. I even started making videos about upcoming donuts and had a good time telling my followers about it.

I love remembering these blissful moments, even while performing the most basic and menial of jobs: whether it was breakfast and a sunrise, or listening to music while handing out donuts to my friends.

But despite these moments, life was still hard. I had hundreds of thousands of followers and two full-time jobs (see below), and every time I saved a little money, something would pop up to take it away. Car trouble, health trouble, life trouble . . . It was always something.

I needed to make more money, so that was the point when I took the job at Chipotle I wrote about earlier: the one I absolutely hated. It was the worst job of them all. I was overworked and underpaid. When I expressed my grievances, my managers gaslit me. The one positive that came out of that time was wearing my Chipotle shirt while making videos about my awful day. It was all in an effort to take an experience I hated and turn it into something funny, to take all the negatives in my life and turn them into something positive. This was a perfect example of the pure good and relief that can come from social media. I remember one time, I was so miserable, sweating behind my mask, and a customer and a coworker were just yammering on and on about the most asinine thing in the world. I thought my head was going to explode. So I went into the bathroom and told the story from my perspective and made it funny. Lots and lots of people were able to relate to an awful day of working at a job you hate.

That was another lesson for me about taking life into your own hands. You can't let work dictate your experiences; you have to dictate it yourself. If Little Caesars says you can only order four Pepperoni Pizza Bites at a time, are you going to just let that be your life? Or are you going to learn how to make them at home, so you can eat more of them, make them taste better, and have them cost a whole lot less? If you want something, you have to take control. Maybe all you need is a little pizza dough, a muffin tin, and a whole bunch of cheese, pepperoni, and garlic butter to turn things around.

PREP TIME: **15 MINUTES, PLUS 30 MINUTES RESTING TIME** COOK TIME: **15 MINUTES** MAKES **6**

LITTLE CAESARS PEPPERONI PIZZA BITES

- 1 tsp olive oil, or nonstick cooking spray
- 12oz (350g) pizza dough from a pizzeria or the grocery store, or 1 Homemade Pizza Dough (page 157), left at room temperature for about 30 minutes
- 12oz (350g) grated low-moisture mozzarella
- 12 large pepperoni slices
- 1 batch Garlic Butter (page 86), warmed

1. Preheat the oven to 400°F (200°F). Use the olive oil to lightly coat the insides of a 6-tin cupcake pan.
2. Use your hands to divide the pizza dough into six pieces, breaking them off and rolling them into balls (don't worry, they don't have to be perfect).
3. Place the first ball into one of the cupcake containers, pressing down with your fingers until the dough covers the bottom of the tin and comes about ¼ of the way up the sides. Repeat with the remaining balls.
4. Evenly distribute half the cheese over the top of each ball. Add the pepperoni, placing two slices into each tin. Top with the remaining cheese. Stir the Garlic Butter and spoon about 1 tablespoon on top of each pizza bite.
5. Bake for about 15 minutes, rotating the pan about halfway through, until the dough is cooked and the cheese is browned.
6. Allow to cool slightly and then enjoy warm. Leftovers can be stored in an airtight container in the refrigerator for up to 1 week.

Note: If you use Homemade Pizza Dough, you will have about 4 ounces (115g) of leftover dough. This can be discarded, or simply rolled out, brushed with some Garlic Butter (page 86) and baked in the oven for a bonus snack.

fast food secrets club

One of the things I was known for early in my social-media career, back in 2023, was something called Fast Food Secrets Club. It was such a fun discovery, and also something that came together totally organically. I've already mentioned the old fast-food jobs I had in the past, and I had a few other friends who worked at different places, like Jack in the Box and Jamba Juice. We started a group text about all the secret-menu items and tricks, like, say, when to show up at Krispy Kreme to get three dozen donuts for free at the end of the night. We called this the Fast Food Secrets Club.

One of the things I learned about over these texts was a pizza place that had a secret code to get 40 percent off your whole order, with no limits whatsoever. We all used it for about a year and a half, and it always worked beautifully. Then one day, I was hanging out with my family and made a video about the code. I basically just threw it out there and went to bed. The post went *catastrophically* viral, basically overnight. When I first posted it, the video had something like fifty thousand views after a couple of hours—solid numbers, but nothing crazy. When I woke up, it had exploded. Within twenty-four hours, it topped out at close to one hundred million views cumulatively between YouTube, Instagram, TikTok, Facebook, and Snapchat. It was wild.

Meanwhile, not only did the code work, it *kept on working*, for something like a year and a half before the Unnamed Very Large Corporation finally deactivated the code. But right away, it was clear that this was really the start of something new for me. People got hooked on Fast Food Secrets Club. I was posting other codes and secret-menu items from friends, but eventually also creating and

“People were jumping into the comments to thank me for how much money my recipes were saving them.”

posting recipes for how to recreate famous fast-food dishes at home. This was a whole new avenue for me in the social-media world, and people were jumping into the comments to thank me for how much money my recipes were saving them.

All of a sudden, I was the president of the Fast Food Secrets Club, sharing codes for discounts on Subway sandwiches, and making dupe recipes for everything from Olive Garden’s fettucine alfredo to the famous Cane’s Sauce from Raising Cane’s—which you’ll find on the next page. It’s absolutely wild to think that my jobs in fast food led to a big social-media presence, and then *that* turned into a recipe in a real-life cookbook that you can hold in your hands. You never know where life is going to take you.

PREP TIME: 1 MINUTE COOK TIME: 5-20 MINUTES SERVES 4-6

½ cup mayo
¼ cup ketchup
½ tsp Worcestershire sauce, plus more as needed
½ tsp garlic powder
½ tsp lemon pepper, plus more as needed
½ tsp fine sea salt, plus more to taste
1lb (454g) bag frozen crinkle-cut french fries
Fry oil (if deep-frying)

CRINKLE-CUT FRIES WITH DUPE CANE'S SAUCE

1. In a medium mixing bowl, add the mayo, ketchup, Worcestershire sauce, garlic powder, lemon pepper, and salt. Whisk until well combined, then season to taste with more lemon pepper and Worcestershire (some people like it stronger than others!). Transfer the sauce into small bowls or ramekins for dipping. Leftovers can be stored in an airtight container for up to 1 week in the refrigerator.
2. Fry your crinkle-cut fries by either air frying or deep-frying:

TO AIR FRY:

1. Preheat the air fryer to 400°F (200°C).
2. In the basket or tray of the air fryer, lay a first batch of french fries in a single layer, making sure not to overcrowd. Cook for 8 minutes, then remove the tray or basket and give them a stir, making sure they stay in a single layer.
3. Return them to the air fryer and cook for 8 to 10 minutes more, until they are crisped to your liking. (Different brands have different cooking times, so keep an eye on them.) Season with salt to taste and eat hot, with the Cane's Sauce.
4. Repeat with the remaining fries and enjoy each batch while still hot.

TO DEEP-FRY:

1. Set up a deep fryer or a deep, heavy-bottomed pot (like a Dutch oven) and fill it with enough fry oil to comfortably fit a layer of fries, with at least 2 inches (5cm) of space from the surface of the oil to the top of the pot to prevent it boiling over.
2. Heat the oil to 375°F (190°C).
3. Once the oil is hot, fry the french fries in batches, being careful not to overcrowd the fryer or pot and drop the temperature too much. Fry for about 90 seconds, until they are a deep golden brown, then lift them out and transfer to a paper towel–lined tray. Season immediately with salt to taste.
4. Repeat with the remaining fries, making sure to return the oil to 375°F (190°C) before adding the next batch. Serve hot, with the Cane's Sauce.

i am not a teacher or a finance bro

Three years after the end of my baseball career, I was up to around three or four million followers across all my social media platforms. I finally quit Chipotle and Krispy Kreme, but my next two jobs were what led me to going into social media full time. The first one, to no one's surprise, was an absolute failure.

You see, I got this job because I had a friend who was a day trader. If you don't know what a day trader is and are curious about it, let me help you out: It's the worst thing ever, please don't do it. Essentially, being a day trader means working in high-volume trading on the stock market, playing with other people's money and taking a commission on the success. My friend was making way more money than I was, and I think he just wanted to help me out and teach me the ropes as a kind of mentor. He hired me to monitor other people's finances and financial positions to make sure they were in order. It was entry level, just as a way to understand how markets work and one day to be able to trade for myself. Essentially, I would get up at 5 a.m., look at the markets, take notes about certain stocks he wanted me to watch, and do some work for his clients. Then I would go and clock in at one of my other jobs: working the slice counter at Flippin' Pizza or, when a slot was available, substitute teaching.

The trader stuff seemed simple enough, but boy, let me tell you: I hated it, and I sucked at it. I even tried to invest what little money I had, using whatever skills I thought I had learned, and I lost it *immediately*. That world is just absolutely not how I'm wired. I would make a play, overthink it, and then find out that if I had waited *literally five more minutes*, I would have made thirty times more money. Thirty! It's incredibly stressful. My nature was fighting me, and I might

Being a baseball player will always be a big part of who I am.

adidas

“

My nature was fighting me, and I might have been the only person in the history of the world who used their teaching money as a way to support their side job as a day trader.

”

have been the only person in the history of the world who used their teaching money as a way to support their side job as a day trader.

Substitute teaching, meanwhile, was a shock to the system in a different way. It turned out that my large number of followers on social media made me really popular with the kids. They were so enthralled with my videos that they actually listened to me in person. Teaching lessons was so much easier, but there was also a complicated side. These kids wanted to be social-media stars. They looked at it as a career path, without realizing that it's a career with no guarantees, stability, or healthcare. Heck, I don't even think it dawned on them that I was *substitute teaching*, so it couldn't have been lucrative. But these kids looked up to me, which made me so afraid; I didn't want to be the spokesperson for social media as a career path. I didn't want to be responsible for driving people into this life. I tried to teach them they should be making videos for fun, not as a path to financial success. I'm not sure if that got through to any of them.

It reached the point that I was offered a brand deal, and I was afraid the kids would see it and think of being a creator as something to aspire to. Construction, movie theater, Krispy Kreme, Angelo's, Chipotle, day trading, substitute teaching . . . I was bouncing from job to job, scraping money together and fighting to do everything I could not to take the plunge. I don't know if I was scared of the idea of leaping into a career that felt so unsafe and unstable. It was everything I was telling the kids not to do. But at the same time, I was kidding myself. It was time to step away from teaching and see what I could really do.

PREP TIME: 30 MINUTES   COOK TIME: 40 MINUTES   SERVES 4-6

If you are making the unsafe choice in your career, it is probably a good idea to make the safe choice in your dinner. Enter: "Seasoned" Chicken and Broccoli Fettucine Alfredo, which is one of my favorite pasta dishes in the world and an absolute crowd-pleaser. Nowadays when I cook a chicken breast properly, like in this recipe, using real seasoning and salt, I can't help but think back to my high school days, when I was eating *nine unseasoned chicken breasts a day*. This is a simple fettucine alfredo, but one that adds protein and a nutritious vegetable.

"SEASONED" CHICKEN AND BROCCOLI FETTUCINE ALFREDO

1½lb (675g) boneless, skinless chicken breasts (see note)
Kosher salt, to taste
Freshly ground black pepper, to taste
1 tsp smoked or plain paprika
1 tsp granulated garlic
1 tsp dried oregano or Italian seasoning
½ tsp granulated onion
Olive or neutral oil, like canola or vegetable
1 head of broccoli, broken into florets
1lb (450g) fettucine pasta
1 stick salted or unsalted butter
3 garlic cloves, finely chopped or grated
1 lemon
¾ cup heavy cream
1 cup freshly grated Parmesan cheese, plus more to garnish
2 tbsp finely chopped parsley leaves

1. Cut the chicken breasts in half horizontally to get maximum crust and seasoning on each piece: Lay one breast flat on a cutting board and press the palm of your nondominant hand down on the chicken. With a sharp knife in your dominant hand, slice horizontally through the middle of the thickest part of the breast, gliding the knife all the way through until you have two pieces of even thickness. Repeat with the remaining breasts. Use paper towels to dry them thoroughly, then season on all sides with salt and pepper, followed by the paprika, granulated garlic, oregano, and granulated onion. Set aside and clean your workstation (and your hands, obviously).
2. Place a large pot of water over high heat and allow it to heat up while you cook the chicken.
3. Heat a medium skillet over medium-high heat. Add enough oil to barely coat the bottom of the pan. On one side of the pan, lay the first seasoned breast down. (If it doesn't sizzle, remove the chicken and wait until the oil is hotter.) Lay down a second breast and allow both to cook for 4 to 5 minutes, until the bottoms are golden brown. Flip them and repeat with the other side, cooking for another 3 to 4 minutes, until cooked through.
4. Remove from the skillet and place on a clean cutting board or a plate to rest. Repeat with the remaining breasts. Keep an eye on the pan, adding more oil when dry. If the spices build up and are burning, wipe the bottom of the pan with a paper towel, then continue cooking. Set the cooked breasts aside.
5. Season the boiling water with plenty of salt (it should taste salty, like a well-seasoned broth). Drop the broccoli into the water and blanch for about 3 minutes, then lift them out with a slotted spoon, spider strainer, or tongs and set aside.
6. To the boiling water, add the fettucine and cook, stirring occasionally, according to the package directions.

RECIPE CONTINUES ON NEXT PAGE

“

It was time to step away from teaching and see what I could really do.

”

7. Meanwhile, set a large skillet or a Dutch oven over medium heat and add the butter. Once melted, add the garlic and cook for about 2 minutes, until just browned around the edges. Grate about three big swipes of zest from the lemon into the pan and stir everything together.
8. Add the cream, a pinch of salt, and a few twists of black pepper. Bring to a simmer, stirring occasionally, then turn off the heat until the pasta is cooked, about 8 to 12 minutes in total.
9. Use tongs to lift the fettucine from the water and add it to the cream sauce. Reserve a mug's worth of the pasta water and set aside.
10. Add the Parmesan cheese and parsley and stir thoroughly. Add the pasta water, ¼ cup at a time, stirring until the noodles are coated in a smooth, creamy sauce. Add a squeeze of lemon juice and season to taste with salt and pepper.
11. Add the broccoli florets and stir everything together one more time. The pasta will thicken as it sits, so keep the pasta water on hand to stir more in if it tightens up before plating.
12. Portion into pasta bowls. Squeeze a little lemon juice over the chicken, cut into slices, lay atop the pasta, and garnish with more Parmesan. Leftovers can be stored in an airtight container in the refrigerator for up to 5 days.

Note: If you don't want to cut your own raw chicken into thin pieces, you can buy them already sliced, or ask the meat counter to do it for you.

the last real job i ever had

I did have one last "real" job: Flippin' Pizza. Good ol' Flippin' was a New York–style pizza chain in San Diego. It was the restaurant job I took right after I quit Chipotle, essentially making minimum wage plus very minimal tips. I still can't believe all the different jobs I had back then, all of them overlapping, coming and going. But Flippin' Pizza will always hold a special place in my heart. I worked the slice counter there, right up front with the people. But just like with Angelo's and Krispy Kreme, I found a part of it that I loved. I was there to reheat slices, work the register, and talk to customers. Most importantly, I got to eat free pizza and watch movies. There was a big TV in the front and a big one in the back, and when the manager left for the day, I could put on any movie I wanted.

All told, I worked at Flippin' Pizza for two years, between 2022 and 2024, working more or fewer hours depending on the other jobs I was cycling through at any given moment. During that time, I signed with a talent manager and had gotten my first brand deal. When they told me how much money it was, I thought they were kidding. It was enough money that I thought I would be set and safe for a long time. I was still living at home with my parents, saving money and helping out my family. So there I was, a guy with a brand deal and a social-media following, all while eating free slices, watching *Men in Black* and *Rush Hour* while on the clock. The truth is, I didn't even need the job at that point, but I enjoyed it so much. It also gave me a little bit of freedom at the back of my mind. It didn't matter if my videos blew up or not, or if another brand deal was ever coming, because no matter what, I knew I was getting a check every two weeks.

> “Most importantly, I got to eat free pizza and watch movies.”

My managers actually begged me to leave Flippin’, and I kept telling them no. I loved it. When I did finally leave, it wasn’t because of social media. My grandma was alive and immunocompromised, and there were still strains of Covid popping up. People would get sick at work, go home for three days, and then come back to work, meaning I was working next to people who still had symptoms, and it just terrified and frustrated me. I couldn’t function with the idea that I might be the reason my grandmother got sick. For that alone, I had to leave. I still miss that job from time to time.

But the good news is that I don’t have to miss the pizza. In fact, I figured out an even better version of their pie that I could make at home. The trick is to use a sheet pan, for a “grandma-style” pie. I still press out the dough nice and thin—but in a sheet pan, no matter what happens, you aren’t making a big mess in your oven or on the counter: Everything is contained right there in the pan. It’s also, I think, a lot easier to shape pizza dough into a sheet pan than it is to toss it up in the air while getting flour all over the kitchen. So, now I’m *still* eating as much pizza as I want, and the nice thing about being home is that I can watch as many movies as I want too.

PREP TIME: 2 HOURS, PLUS 24–48 HOURS   COOK TIME: 12 MINUTES   SERVES 4–6

THIN-CRUST SHEET-PAN PEPPERONI PIZZA

For the Homemade Pizza Dough

1 tsp honey
1 tsp active dry yeast
2 tbsp olive oil, plus more for brushing
4½ cups all-purpose flour
4¼ cups bread flour
4 tsp fine sea salt

For the Basic Pizza Sauce

28oz (794g) can whole peeled tomatoes, drained (see note)
1 garlic clove, grated or finely chopped
1 tsp olive oil
½ tsp dried oregano
Freshly ground black pepper, to taste
Kosher or fine sea salt, to taste

For the Pizza

Olive oil, for greasing and for garnish
1 Homemade Pizza Dough, at room temperature for about 30 minutes, covered
1 batch Basic Pizza Sauce
1lb (450g) grated low-moisture mozzarella
10oz (300g) "cup and crisp" pepperoni
1 cup grated Parmesan cheese
Thinly sliced fresh basil (optional)

HOMEMADE PIZZA DOUGH

1. To the bowl of a stand mixer fitted with a dough hook or to a large bowl if mixing by hand, add 2¾ cups warm water. Add the honey and stir gently, then sprinkle the yeast over the top. Allow it to sit for a few minutes until the yeast is foaming and activated. (If it doesn't activate, your yeast is old and should be discarded.)
2. Add the olive oil, all-purpose flour, and bread flour and mix on medium-low speed for about 6 minutes (or knead by hand for about 8 minutes). The dough should start to come together and feel cohesive. Remove the dough from the hook and lay it in the bottom of the bowl, then cover with plastic wrap and let rest for about 20 minutes at room temperature.
3. Add the salt and mix on medium for 3 minutes (or knead by hand for about 6 minutes). It should feel cohesive and not overly sticky. Divide the dough into three even portions. Shape into balls by holding the dough in your hands and stretching it into a ball, like you're stuffing a sock into itself, using your fingers to stretch one side and curling it inward with your fingers. The goal is to create a tightly stretched ball with a smooth top (this will be the top of your dough). "Close" the bottom of the dough by twisting and tightly pinching the dough.
4. Place the dough on a lightly oiled baking sheet with the smooth top facing up. Repeat with the other balls. Lightly oil the tops of the doughs and cover the whole sheet with plastic wrap.
5. For best results, allow the dough balls to chill in the refrigerator for 24 to 48 hours (also known as "cold fermenting"). The longer the cold ferment, the more complex the dough flavor will be, but the visual cues will be similar. They can be taken out and warmed on the counter for 1 hour before baking, or placed in a freezer bag and frozen for up to 3 months.

RECIPE CONTINUES ON NEXT PAGE

BASIC PIZZA SAUCE

1. In a bowl, place the tomatoes and use your hands to crush them thoroughly, removing and discarding any hard stems or leftover pieces of skin.
2. Add the garlic, olive oil, oregano, a few twists of black pepper, and a pinch of salt. Taste for salt and pepper and adjust seasoning as desired.

Note: For a no-waste sauce, reserve the juice from the can of tomatoes for use in soups and pasta sauces.

PIZZA

1. Position an oven rack in the center and preheat the oven to 500°F (260°C) or as high as it goes. If you have a gas oven, remove the bottom rack as well (and skip step 6).
2. Drizzle the olive oil into a 13 x 18-inch (33 x 46cm) sheet pan and use your hands to spread it across the bottom and sides.
3. Uncover the pizza dough and lay it on a clean work surface, like your kitchen counter, with the oiled sheet pan next to it. With your hands still oiled, use light, confident pressure to press your fingers into the dough, shaping it into roughly the same size as the sheet pan. Lift the edges as needed and stretch the dough, like you're putting on a bed sheet, while being careful to avoid rips. Once the dough is even and close enough to the right shape, lay it into the sheet pan (keeping the smooth "top" of the dough still facing up). Shape the dough into the pan, getting it as close to the edges as you can.
4. Cover the sheet pan with plastic wrap and allow the dough to proof for 30 minutes to 1 hour. The dough will relax and get softer. Gently lift the edges with your fingers and try to spread the dough closer to the edges of the pan.
5. Spread the pizza sauce across the dough in an even layer, followed by the mozzarella. Be sure to place a little more cheese along the edges of the pan to yield crispier, cheesy edges. Spread the pepperoni across the top of the pizza in an even layer, then sprinkle with half the Parmesan.
6. Bake for about 10 minutes, until the top of the pizza is golden brown and the pepperoni is starting to char at the edges. Use a spatula to carefully lift up the edge of the pizza and check the bottom; if it's golden brown, the pizza is done. If not, continue to bake, checking every 1 to 2 minutes. Skip to step 8.
7. Alternatively, if you have a gas oven, lay the sheet pan directly on the bottom of the oven—this will brown the bottom super fast. Bake until the bottom of the crust is golden brown, but check often as it will burn quickly.
8. Remove the pizza from the oven, then top with the remaining Parmesan. Use a spatula to lift the pizza from the pan and onto a cutting board. Cut into six squares, then top with the basil (if using). Drizzle with fresh olive oil and serve. Leftovers can be stored in an airtight container in the refrigerator for up to 5 days.

Note: If you want to make multiple pizzas, it is very easy to do if you have multiple sheet pans. Then all you have to do is prepare all the doughs and you can just top them and bake them one right after the other.

discovering a community

Suddenly, I was a full-time social-media creator. It was my only job. I accepted an offer to go to a football game in New York as a YouTube ambassador to make a speech for brand ambassadors before the game. They put me in a luxury suite to watch the game, and a dad and his kids approached me to tell me how excited they were to meet me.

I'm not a guy who goes out a ton, so this was one of the first examples of looking at these numbers in my phone and all of a sudden realizing how many different kinds of people were following along and enjoying my content. I heard from people in real life, young and old, putting real faces to some of those numbers.

I even started releasing merchandise and little recipe books, and suddenly this hobby became more than just a bunch of viral videos. It was a real and effective way to connect with people. I'd created a community that people wanted to be a part of. This level of support is what led me to doing my TEDx Talk in Canada, where I discovered that people were *flying all the way there* just to see me speak live. My fame was becoming international in a way I never could have dreamed.

You have to be careful, though, about finding community in a comment section. It's a funny thing: On social media, you *become* successful by communicating with the few people who are first paying attention, reading their comments and seeing what's working and what's not. I was getting over five million views on most videos, with so many comments that I couldn't really dive into feedback like I used to. I had to choose not to get too wrapped up in the comments; otherwise, that could start to negatively affect the work I was doing. If I read the comments, I was afraid I would start overthinking it, instead of staying true to my own internal barometer. I always care

"Comments sections are like food—too much of it is incredibly, deeply bad for you."

about what people are saying and how they're reacting, but I can't let their opinions hinder or drive the creative process behind the videos I want to make.

Comments sections are like food—too much of it is incredibly, deeply bad for you, no matter how "nutritious" some of those comments or bites might be. There's a limit to how much one can observe them without it being unhealthy. I still try to read a handful of comments, just to get a sense of the overall vibe, and then I have to cut myself off and move on. Once a post grows to millions and millions of views, you have to be smart about how you interact. Protecting yourself emotionally and mentally while also staying open to listening and adjusting is a delicate balance. The early days of the Fast Food Secrets Club, for example, were a special time with a smaller community that I look back on with such fondness.

PREP TIME: 20 MINUTES COOK TIME: 15 MINUTES MAKES 12

I think breakfast lovers are their own kind of community: passionate people who say it's their favorite meal and will eat it morning, noon, or night. So here is my entry, held up humbly for the breakfast community to enjoy. To me, combining pancakes and bacon is the ultimate fusion dish: Cooked bacon is dipped in pancake batter and griddled, topped with powdered sugar, and served with a side dip of maple syrup. I'm telling you, these are outrageously good, and in a pinch, you can even bring them in the car and eat them as an on-the-go snack, if you don't mind dripping a little bit of maple syrup.

BACON PANCAKES

1 cup all-purpose flour
2 tbsp granulated white sugar
1 tbsp baking powder
¼ tsp fine sea salt
1 cup whole milk
2 tbsp canola oil
1 egg
2 tbsp salted butter, divided
12 crispy cooked bacon strips, preferably hickory smoked
¼ cup powdered sugar
Maple syrup, to serve

1. Preheat a skillet, ideally cast-iron, over medium heat or preheat a griddle to 350°F (180°C).
2. In a large mixing bowl, combine the flour, sugar, baking powder, and salt. Whisk until well combined.
3. In a medium bowl, combine the milk, oil, and egg, and whisk until fully combined. To the large bowl with the dry ingredients, add the wet ingredients and whisk together until well mixed.
4. Now it's time to make Bacon Pancakes, but be warned—this can get a little messy and drippy . . . but that's part of the fun, right? In the skillet or on the griddle, place 1 tablespoon of the butter and tilt the skillet to distribute across the bottom. Using tongs, dip the first slice of bacon into the batter, then lift, allowing the excess batter to drip off. Lay the bacon in the pan and cook for about 1 minute, until browned on the bottom. Flip and repeat with the other side, another 45 to 60 seconds.
5. Adjust the temperature of your stove based on how this "tester" turns out (i.e., if it's a pale brown, increase the heat). Repeat with the remaining bacon, adding more butter to the pan as needed and working in batches until all are cooked. Transfer to a serving platter or individual plates.
6. Using a fine-mesh strainer, generously dust the powdered sugar over the bacon pancakes. Serve with the maple syrup on the side and enjoy immediately. Leftovers can be frozen in an airtight container for up to 2 months and reheated in the oven.

with great power . . .

Admiration and, frankly, attention have always made me incredibly nervous and scared. The more people I made proud, the more people I could let down.

When I was at that football game, confronted joyfully by a dad and his kids, I kept it together and smiled, thanked them, and talked about how amazing my job and life were. Right after that exchange, I went to the bathroom. Unlike what I'm most well-known for, I did not stand in the mirror and make a video. Instead, I locked myself in the stall and sat there for twenty-five minutes, having a full panic attack: rapid breathing, nausea, cold chills, and claustrophobia. It was touching to realize that every like on a post represents a person, but it also suddenly became very real how many people I was reaching. The numbers had faces and ages and personalities. Children were watching me and telling their dads. I wanted to make them all proud, and I was being crushed under the weight of my own fears.

I eventually calmed down and left that public bathroom. I pulled myself together and moved forward, because what else could I do? Either I had to grow and evolve, or I was going to just collapse in on myself. With reach comes responsibility. I decided that while everything I posted wasn't done haphazardly or flippantly, I needed the stories I shared to have liability, importance, and weight to them too. I had to make sure that I was a force for good and not just for attention and success. My audience had to live in my head when I made videos. There were children looking up to me, people who could, frankly, be influenced. I tried to imagine a young, impressionable me watching these videos. How would I react to them? I needed to be there for them. I wanted to be a comfort food.

“

I had to make sure that I was a force for good and not just for attention and success.

”

PREP TIME: 10 MINUTES, PLUS 3–12 HOURS MARINATING TIME (SEE NOTE) COOK TIME: 45 MINUTES SERVES 6

This recipe is a *deep* comfort food for me: classic clam chowder with bacon, celery, garlic, and potatoes. But I have also added my own flair, as usual, and it involves building a ton of flavor on top of a basic pack of saltine crackers, turning them into Old Bay saltines, which soak up extra flavor and fat overnight, then get rebaked until they become unbelievably delicious. They are amazing on their own or dipped or crumbled into your clam chowder.

BACON AND CLAM CHOWDER WITH OLD BAY SALTINES

½ cup plus 1 tbsp olive or neutral oil, such as canola or vegetable, divided
2 tsp Old Bay seasoning
1 tsp granulated garlic
½ tsp paprika
Two 8oz (227g) sleeves of saltine crackers
5 slices of thick-cut bacon, roughly diced
1 small yellow onion, or ½ large onion, diced
3 celery stalks, diced
2 garlic cloves, finely chopped
Kosher or fine sea salt, to taste
Freshly ground black pepper, to taste
1 tbsp all-purpose flour
1 tsp dried Italian seasoning
1 dried bay leaf
2 cups heavy cream
Three 6½oz (184g) cans chopped clams (packed in clam juice)
8oz (237ml) bottle clam juice
1lb (450g) Yukon gold potatoes, diced
Hot sauce, to serve

Note: To get ahead on this, the Old Bay saltines need to be left in the seasoning mixture for at least 3 hours, or overnight, before being baked off. It's a great trick, because the saltines get a big hit of flavor and become extra decadent after being rebaked with the additional oil. You can get creative and add other seasonings instead, like ranch powder or Cajun seasoning.

1. In a large ziplock bag or a resealable container, add ½ cup of the oil, the Old Bay, granulated garlic, and paprika. Mix until well combined, then add the saltines and toss gently until the crackers are fully coated in the spice mixture.
2. Seal the bag or container and lay flat at room temperature for at least 3 hours and up to 12 hours.
3. When you are ready to cook, preheat the oven to 250°F (130°C).
4. On two baking sheets, arrange the saltines in a single layer. Bake on separate racks for 15 minutes, then remove from the oven and set aside to cool to room temperature.
5. Place a heavy-bottomed pot or a Dutch oven on the stove over medium heat. Add the remaining 1 tablespoon olive oil and the bacon. Cook for about 5 minutes, stirring occasionally, until most of the fat is rendered but the bacon is not quite crispy yet.
6. Add the onion, celery, garlic, a pinch of salt, and several twists of freshly ground black pepper. Stir and cook for about 8 minutes, until the onions are just tender.
7. Add the flour, Italian seasoning, and bay leaf and allow the flour to toast for about 90 seconds, stirring frequently. Stirring constantly, add half the cream a few tablespoons at a time. Once it is bubbling, add the rest of the cream, followed by the clams and clam juice.
8. Stir in the potatoes and another pinch of salt. Increase the heat to medium-high and bring to a strong simmer, stirring frequently. Cover the pot, reduce the heat to a gentle simmer, and cook for 15 to 20 minutes, until the potatoes are tender but not falling apart.
9. Season with salt and black pepper to taste. Serve with the Old Bay saltines and the hot sauce. Leftover soup can be stored in an airtight container in the refrigerator for up to 3 days. Leftover saltines can last in an airtight container at room temperature for up to 5 days.

the power of leverage

The first time I was offered a brand deal back in late 2023, when I was still working at Angelo's, the payout was more money than I could really imagine. Let's just say it was enough that I could buy a car and cover my parents' rent for three years. I won't say who the brand was, but the amount of money would obviously have been life-changing for me in that moment. But I had to take a deep breath and look at it honestly. I knew that I did not align with the brand. I didn't believe in what they stood for, so I said no to the money.

It was a pivotal moment between me and my manager. He had negotiated this tremendous amount of money, and there I was, telling him we weren't going to take it. I told him I needed to protect my audience, but that I also needed to protect myself. I decided then and there that no amount of money was worth dishonoring the relationship between myself and my fanbase. When I said no, it was like a weight was lifted from my shoulders. Just saying no was maybe the happiest I'd ever felt in any business transaction. I was walking away from more money than I had ever seen, but I believed in myself, my audience, and my ability to continue to grow and trust in that relationship.

Three years later, we now say no to brand deals all the time. They might be clothing brands, food companies, anything. We say no way more often than we say yes, and it's because of that sense of responsibility. It's funny, because these brands, or more specifically the third-party companies charged with finding influencer deals, are not used to hearing no and usually think we're using a negotiation tactic. But when you say no for *moral* reasons and you explain that to them, they don't know how to respond. To be honest, there have been times when the negotiators came back and got moody, emotional, or even threatening: "If you say no, we will never, ever work with you." We say no anyway.

They always come back. They come back because they want us more than we want them, and I'm confident that bigger and better offers will come because the relationship with my fans is pure and based on respect. I will never tell anyone to buy something or do something that I wouldn't do myself. That's the bare minimum. I became who I am because of my values, and I couldn't just abandon them for money. I'm a staunch advocate for standing firm and sticking to your ideals.

When it comes to making business decisions in this new world of sponsored content creation, there is no syllabus. There is no guidebook (unless you count this as one). You need to go with your gut, follow your instincts, and try some new things to see what works. As of this writing, some of those fun new things have included traveling around the world to film myself trying viral foods. I have found that if I get stuck, I try something new, and then the easier path just opens up for me. When I trust the process, it tends to work out.

That was what lead me to this recipe. I had tried stir-fried lobster noodles at restaurants and loved them, but when I'm cooking at home, as opposed to a fancy restaurant kitchen, breaking down a whole lobster is just not feasible. Instead, I found another way: I discovered that I could do it with a simple can of jumbo lump crabmeat and the whole world became brighter, easier, and more delicious. This recipe is *way* easier than it should be, considering how delicious it is. Just trust the process.

PREP TIME: 5 MINUTES COOK TIME: 15 MINUTES SERVES 4–6

STIR-FRIED CRAB NOODLES WITH SCALLIONS, GINGER, AND GARLIC

- 1 tsp bouillon powder (or omit, if you are salt-sensitive)
- 3 tbsp oyster sauce
- 1½ tbsp soy sauce
- 2 tsp granulated white sugar
- 6 scallions, trimmed, white and light-green parts thinly sliced, dark-green parts cut into 1in (2.5cm) pieces
- 3 tbsp peeled and finely chopped fresh ginger
- 6 garlic cloves, smashed and roughly chopped
- 1lb (450g) fresh Chinese noodles, such as egg noodles or lo mein, or 12oz (350g) dried Chinese noodles or spaghetti
- 2 tbsp neutral oil, such as canola or vegetable
- 12oz (350g) canned jumbo lump crabmeat, drained
- 1 tsp toasted sesame oil (optional)

1. Place a large pot of water over high heat and bring to a boil.
2. Meanwhile, in a medium mixing bowl, add ¾ cup warm water and stir in the bouillon powder. Add the oyster sauce, soy sauce, and sugar. Stir well to combine and set aside.
3. To a medium bowl, add the white and light-green scallions along with the ginger and garlic. Set aside.
4. Cook the noodles according to the package directions, but remove them from the heat about 30 seconds before they are done. Drain and set aside.
5. Place a large wok or a wide skillet over medium-high heat. Add the oil and, once it is shimmering, add the ginger-garlic-scallion mixture. Fry for about 30 seconds, stirring frequently, until the mixture begins to brown at the edges.
6. Pour in the sauce mixture and bring to a simmer. Add the crab and bring back to a simmer, about 30 seconds more.
7. Add the noodles (see note), along with the scallion greens. Stir rapidly and, once it is sizzling and fully combined, turn off the heat. Drizzle with the sesame oil (if using) and stir one more time. Serve immediately. Leftovers can be stored in an airtight container in the refrigerator for up to 4 days.

Note: If the noodles have clumped together by the time you're ready to add them to the pan, run them under warm tap water to loosen, then drain.

you don't change, the people around you do

Be careful of thinking for other people: You might make them smarter than they actually are.

In 2024, I made the Forbes list, and they valued my net worth at five million dollars. This was not true. Not in the least. But I found that people started trying to think for me. People saw the success I had and assumed it meant I was winning at life to a much higher degree than the reality. Now look—I was making more money than I ever had in my life, but people were definitely assuming it was that Forbes five million. But that's what happens when fame gets involved: Even if it's not a number in a magazine, people tend to assume that famous people are doing better than they might be.

For me, I really didn't feel any different. The faster my success grew, the more normal I felt about the change. I went about my routine, waking up and going to work in the same ways. Maybe I felt a little bit less stressed about where my next meal or rent money was coming from, but the vast majority of my day was exactly the same as it was before. The people who only saw the numbers and views going up often assumed that I must have changed as well. All they saw was a successful person who looked like the person they used to know.

When people see me doing a collaboration video with a movie star—I do these for free by the way—they suddenly equate me to being on the same playing field as a celebrity. But making a video with a movie star does not make you a movie star.

People want to be a part of the ride I'm on. They start by quietly alluding to the money I must have. They talk about how long they've known me, or how they remember my mom, or whatever else, to try to set up for the ask. "Hey, I have a movie script. Do you think you can pass this to somebody for me?" "I have these bills coming up . . . " "I've got this business opportunity . . . " They sell me on how tight our relationship is, even if it never really was in the first place. To play devil's advocate, I want to point out that the people who do this don't understand how many other people are asking me for things all the time. For them, it's a singular action, asking me for one favor. They don't know that they were the fifth person to hit me up that morning.

I hate disappointing people, so the only solution that has made sense is to insulate myself. I became afraid of having relationships. I wanted to help people, but I couldn't handle doing it in a public setting. If I was generating my own videos, I had more control over what I was presenting, but out in the real world, it was much harder for me to compartmentalize my emotions. So, I became inaccessible, afraid of making new friends or keeping old ones. I told myself, "Don't go to that dinner. Don't go to that get-together. Seclude yourself." That was my solution, and it was not sustainable, even though it worked for a time. I became a guy in his own bubble, making videos, connecting with millions of people online but fewer and fewer people in real life.

When I wouldn't let anyone else in, I always turned back to the kitchen. That was where I could calm down and do things just for myself. There was something tangible and tactile in the kitchen. I could hold a knife. I could pound a chicken breast. I could work at my own speed and live in my own world. When you're in your lowest moments, a dish like chicken Parm will be there for you. You could say that I protected myself in a delicious garlicky breadcrumb, snuggling in a bath of cheese and tomato.

PREP TIME: 35 MINUTES, PLUS 1–12 HOURS RESTING TIME   COOK TIME: 20 MINUTES   SERVES 4

GARLIC-BREADED CHICKEN PARM

- 4 boneless, skinless chicken breasts (ideally about 6oz / 175g each)
- 8oz (225g) panko breadcrumbs
- 1 full head of garlic, peeled and finely chopped
- 2 tbsp granulated garlic, divided
- 1 tbsp dried oregano
- 1½ cups all-purpose flour
- Kosher or fine sea salt
- Freshly ground black pepper
- 3 eggs
- Fry oil, such as canola, vegetable, or peanut
- 1 batch Basic Tomato Sauce (page 121), warmed, or one 24oz (680g) jar of your preferred sauce
- 8oz (225g) fresh mozzarella, sliced
- Freshly grated Parmesan cheese, for the topping and to garnish

1. Butterfly and pound out your chicken breasts: Place the first breast flat on a cutting board. Place your nondominant palm on top of the breast to steady it, then slice horizontally through the center of the thickest part of the breast until you are about 1 inch (2.5cm) from the back. Open it like a book, slicing the "spine" in any places necessary to help flatten the breast to an even thickness. Repeat with the remaining chicken breasts.
2. Lay a long sheet of plastic wrap on a work surface. Lay the first chicken breast on the plastic wrap, then cover it with another sheet of plastic. Using a meat mallet or a heavy bottomed pot, pound the breast with medium force, until about ⅛ to ¼ inch (3 to 5mm) thick. Set aside and repeat with the remaining breasts.
3. In a wide plate or bowl, combine the panko, chopped garlic, 1 tablespoon of the granulated garlic, and the dried oregano. Stir to combine and spread the breadcrumb mixture out into an even layer. To another wide plate or bowl, add the flour, as well as 2 teaspoons salt, the remaining 1 tablespoon granulated garlic, and several twists of black pepper. In a third wide plate or bowl, combine the eggs, a pinch of salt, and 1 tablespoon water and whisk until well combined.
4. Line up your breading station: Place the chicken at one end, followed by the flour, egg, breadcrumbs, and finally a baking sheet. Season the chicken breasts all over with salt, then use the wet hand–dry hand method (keeping one hand wet and one dry) to start breading the chicken.
5. Using your dry hand, lay the first breast into the flour mixture, flipping over until fully coated. Shake off the excess, then drop into the egg mixture. Use your wet hand to flip it over until fully coated. Lift up and let the excess egg drain off, then transfer to the breadcrumb mixture. Use your dry hand again to cover the breast with breadcrumbs, patting slightly as you go. Lift and transfer to the baking sheet. Repeat with the remaining breasts. For best results, chill the breaded breasts in the refrigerator for at least 1 hour but ideally overnight. This really helps the breading to adhere to the chicken after cooking.

RECIPE CONTINUES ON NEXT PAGE

6. When you are ready to cook, set up a deep fryer or a heavy bottomed pot like a Dutch oven, and fill it with enough fry oil to comfortably fit the chicken, ensuring there are at least 2 inches (5cm) of space from the surface of the oil to the top of the pot to prevent it boiling over. Heat the oil to 325°F (160°C).
7. Once the oil is hot, fry the chicken breasts, one at a time, doing your best to maintain the oil temperature. Fry for about 4 minutes, until deep golden brown, then transfer to a paper towel-lined tray. Repeat with the remaining breasts, making sure to return the oil to 325°F (160°C) before adding more chicken.
8. Once the chicken is cooked, place an oven rack one position below the very top and turn on the broiler. Place the chicken breasts onto a clean baking sheet and add a spoonful of the tomato sauce across the tops of each breast. Divide the sliced mozzarella evenly over the chicken pieces and top with a generous amount of the Parmesan cheese. Broil for 1 to 2 minutes, rotating the pan and chicken pieces as needed, until the cheese is browned and bubbling.
9. Ladle some of the warmed tomato sauce onto four serving plates and lay the finished chicken parm on top. Finish with more fresh Parmesan and serve immediately. Leftovers can be stored in an airtight container in the refrigerator for up to 5 days.

reacting to fame

People react to fame very differently. I have seen some people react by having total, reckless abandon for any decisions they make, like they're living in a bubble. These are the kind of people who are so overwhelmed by the chaos that is fame and judgment that they just throw all caution to the wind and do whatever they want. That is more of the rock star mentality.

Then there's how I deal with fame, which is to become hyperaware of the people around me and what I'm doing, and to insulate myself as a means of self-protection.

Or to put it another way: If you were a kid who had a birthday party and somehow ended up with two hundred extra dollars, what would you do with it? Would you splurge and spend it all, or would you put it in a savings account?

I am very clearly the savings-account kid, and this new life, whatever it represented, added to the pressure I already put on myself. I didn't celebrate my success but instead worried about how to maintain the momentum. How do I sustain this career? How do I grow as a person? How do I take care of my family *and* myself?

But as time went by, it was clear that I needed to learn how to live life more comfortably, not from a financial standpoint but rather from an *emotional* one. I had to constantly check in with myself: How do I operate my life with more intention? How do I flow through the world with more calmness and assuredness? How do I savor the moments when I can? Instead of being stressed out by all the people coming out of the woodwork to ask for money or help, how do I go and find the people I want to help? I wanted to be the driving force in my life, not the one reacting to everyone else coming at me. I love to

"I wanted to be the driving force in my life, not the one reacting to everyone else coming at me."

help people without broadcasting it, whether that is through extreme overtipping, giving to causes I care about, or donating the extravagant things that brands offer me. Attention, to me, ruins a good deed: I wanted all to myself the quiet, warm feeling that comes from giving to others.

I also want to be very clear: The positives of fame, at whatever level I have it, *far, far* outweigh the negatives. The good feelings eclipse the bad. I love when I get to tip two hundred dollars on a twenty-dollar tab, or donate money to causes and communities I care about.

I could never, for instance, enjoy a whole tray of homemade Pop-Tarts. But making it and sharing it with others is an incredible feeling. Context affects flavor, so to speak, and knowing that someone is biting into something that you made, with the flour you chose, made from dough you worked with your own hands, makes it feel better. It is the most satisfying way.

HOMEMADE POP-TARTS

For the Pie Crust

Makes 2 portions

2½ cups all-purpose flour, plus more

2 tsp granulated white sugar

1 tsp fine sea salt

2 sticks unsalted butter, chilled and cubed

For the Pop-Tarts

12oz (350g) pie-crust dough, homemade or store-bought, at room temperature

1 tbsp all-purpose flour, plus more for dusting

½ cup tightly packed light or dark brown sugar

2½ tsp ground cinnamon, divided

A pinch of granulated salt

1 egg

2 tsp plus 1 tbsp milk, divided

¾ cup powdered sugar, sifted

¼ tsp vanilla extract

PIE CRUST

1. To the bowl of a stand mixer fitted with the paddle attachment, add the flour, sugar, and salt and beat on low speed to incorporate.
2. Add the butter and gradually increase the speed to medium, beating for about 3 minutes, until the butter is broken up and no pieces are larger than a pea.
3. Continue running the mixer and slowly pour in ½ cup ice water a little bit at a time, using as much as needed for the dough to come together. If you run out of water and the dough is still crumbly, add about 1 tablespoon more at a time.
4. Turn the dough out onto a clean work surface and knead for about 10 seconds, then wrap it tightly in plastic wrap and transfer to the refrigerator until ready to use. The dough is best used within 2 to 3 days but will keep in the freezer, tightly wrapped in plastic wrap, for up to 6 months.

POP-TARTS

1. Preheat the oven to 375°F (190°C).
2. Divide the dough in half. On a lightly floured surface, use a floured rolling pin to roll out each half so they are about ⅛ inch (5mm) thick. Lay them on top of each other and cut into a square roughly 8 x 8 inches (20 x 20cm). (Leftover dough can be frozen or discarded.)
3. On a baking sheet lined with parchment paper, place 1 dough square in the center. In a small mixing bowl, add the flour, brown sugar, 2 teaspoons of the cinnamon, and a pinch of salt. Whisk to combine, then spread across the center of the dough, leaving about 1 inch (2.5cm) of space around the border. Lay the other piece of dough on top, then use the tines of a fork to crimp and seal the edges all the way around the perimeter. Use your fork to evenly poke holes across the top of the dough. I like to make eight even rows, with four stabs per row.
4. In another small bowl, whisk together the egg with 2 teaspoons of the milk. Use a brush to baste the top of the Pop-Tart with the egg mixture.
5. Bake for about 15 minutes, until golden and cooked through.
6. Meanwhile, in a small mixing bowl, combine the powdered sugar, the remaining 1 tablespoon milk, the remaining ½ teaspoon cinnamon, and the vanilla extract. Whisk to combine. It should be spreadable but not watery. Adjust thickness as needed with more milk or powdered sugar.
7. Once the Pop-Tart is cooked, remove from the oven. If the glaze has seized up at all and is too thick to brush, add a small splash of milk and stir. Brush the glaze across the top of the warm tart and let it sit for 5 minutes, until the glaze is set. Cut the tart in half down the center, then cut each half into three equal rectangles for a total of six rectangles. Enjoy immediately, or store in an airtight container for up to 1 week to eat cold or refreshed in a toaster oven.

a support system is important after all

Back in my baseball days, I prided myself on being independent. I didn't ask for help and did everything on my own. I was putting my body through the absolute worst pain and rejected anybody who came by offering help. This method was so heavily ingrained in my brain for so long. I had been taught to be my own overused hype beast, because nobody was coming to save me and I had to support myself. To think that I was ever actually able to do anything on my own was arrogant, and also narcissistic.

As I've gotten older, I've realized the power in asking for help. While my mom taught me that how you ask matters, I have since matured enough to realize the there is also a difference between what you want and what you need. It is only in the last year or so, as a twenty-eight-year-old, that I discovered my true need is to surround myself with real friends, with the people who allow me to be myself, who I can say no to without it affecting our relationship. I wanted to come home and leave my social-media life at the door.

I've learned who my important friends are, the ones who remain their honest selves when they are in unique circumstances, no matter how fancy or bizarre a place I might drag them to. Because for my support group, what I really need is to be surrounded by the people

"For my support group, what I really need is to be surrounded by the people who tether me to reality."

who tether me to reality, even if the things I'm doing for work seem so far removed. Walking down a red carpet is not normal. Flying to Florence to make a gelato video is not normal. But when I have the ability to fly a friend out to do the gig with me or to be my plus-one for a movie premiere, I want to have that safety of them being them, and that they not treat me any differently than they would if we were sitting on the couch watching TV. We can just be ourselves and have fun. Having these relationships protects me from the total abnormality of what else is going on in the world around me. Without normalcy, the whole universe feels like it's spinning out of control. It's a strange thing, if you think about it, to ask your friends to do you a favor by just being themselves. I want nothing from them other than to be the people I trust and love.

PREP TIME: **5 MINUTES** COOK TIME: **15 MINUTES** MAKES **6**

This recipe is a collection of normal things, brought together for a great time: a package of ready-made mini graham-cracker pie crusts, a couple of Hershey's chocolate bars, some mini marshmallows, and little bit of chocolate-chip cookie dough. It's just a handful of store-bought ingredients, laid onto a baking sheet in a particular order, and baked for less than 15 minutes, and the result is absolute magic.

MINI COOKIE S'MORE PIES

1 package Keebler Ready Crust Mini Graham Cracker Pie Crusts (see note)
Two 1.55oz (43g) chocolate bars, such as Hershey's
1 cup mini marshmallows
6oz (175g) chocolate-chip cookie dough, such as Nestlé Toll House

1. Preheat the oven to 350°F (180°C).
2. Lay the pie crusts on a baking sheet. Break up the chocolate bars into squares and divide them evenly between all six crusts. Divide the marshmallows evenly over the top of each.
3. Next, divide the cookie dough—you're looking for about 2 tablespoons per portion. Use your hands to mold the dough over the top of the crusts, enclosing the chocolate and marshmallows and forming a seal all the way around.
4. Bake for 12 to 14 minutes, until the cookies are just barely done. Remove from the oven and let cool for a few minutes before eating. Leftovers can be stored in an airtight container for up to 5 days.

Note: Rather than buying premade pie-crust dough, use the recipe featured in Homemade Pop-Tarts on page 181.

accepting the new version of your life

One of the key steps to growing up for me has been realizing that my old life is not coming back. There's no going back to the pizza shop to watch movies and sling slices. The impact that I had on people, my life, or the person I was before is gone. There are obviously a lot of people in the world who don't know who I am, but I am always a few moments from someone meeting me for the first time with a lot of preloaded information in their head of what they know about me.

The acceptance part is understanding that those kinds of encounters aren't a bad thing—they're just part of change. Regular, inevitable change comes in every form, shape, and size. It's part of life: People come and go; there are health scares, deaths, financial changes, career changes. It's all on the table. How you react to it is the secret. I'm still known by that goofy name I typed in as a kid, "Jordan the Stallion," a name I still try to avoid as much as I can. But I also need to fully admit that that persona is what I created and will forever be tied to who I am. It will be the first line in my obituary, and it would be absurd to pretend otherwise. At the same time, these opportunities have made my life a whole lot easier. I talk differently than I used to, and I move differently. Once I accepted and embraced the truth of these changes—both positive and negative—it made my life a lot more fun.

The first time I took my mom to the state fair was also the first time I'd gone to a public place since my followership had really grown to that crazy level—I had about 15 million followers by that point. Things were different now, and it was applying to real life. Somebody came up asking for a picture. Then a second person came, then ten, then twenty. It escalated quickly and shocked us. We'd never experienced anything like that before. My mom is a small woman, and it got scary very quickly. Lines started forming all around us, and I didn't see a way to get my mom out of there. Security literally had to escort us out. It made me want to turn inward emotionally and also physically isolate myself from the world. I didn't go on dates. I didn't go to concerts. I stayed secluded because I was afraid of being seen only as the happy, enthusiastic, public-facing persona who eats food and throws his glasses across the room in excitement. I saw people turning their cameras toward me, and I didn't want any part of it.

I had not yet embraced or understood all that had changed. These days, I've come to terms with my circumstances. For example, on a recent trip to London, I really wanted to see a Shakespeare play with my friends. I knew that the moment I walked outside, people would be taking out their cameras. But I wanted to go anyway. So, I went. And instead of fighting the inevitable, I embraced it. I talked to people, posed for pictures. Then we settled into our seats, and we all became part of this same community, there to watch a play together. When I leaned into the reality of the fame, I was able to harness it rather than be frightened of it. I got what I wanted: an enjoyable moment with my loved ones.

I've managed these experiences by being intentional. That doesn't mean I go anywhere I want. But I know that if I simply cannot give an activity or commitment my full attention, then I will avoid it. When I am prepared to embrace the reality of the public reaction, I know it will all work out. It's like riding the wave instead of swimming against it. As a guy who never felt comfortable, I love feeling like I've made people feel comfortable enough to come talk to me. I'm always me, whether I'm home on the couch in sweats, or all dressed up for a big night on the town.

PREP TIME: 2 MINUTES COOK TIME: 7 MINUTES SERVES 1

Just because you want to have a simple sweatpants kind of night at home doesn't mean that your Top Ramen can't get a little dressed up for you. This is Top Ramen 2.0, with extra protein from a runny egg yolk, some simple greens, and the most delicious mushrooms you'll ever make. All dressed up, but easy enough for a quiet night on the couch.

DRESSED-UP RAMEN WITH SOY-BUTTERED MUSHROOMS

- 1 tbsp salted or unsalted butter
- 2 tsp soy sauce
- 1 cup thinly sliced mushrooms, such as shiitake
- 1 scallion, thinly sliced, green and white parts separated
- 2 cups loosely packed baby spinach leaves
- 3oz (85g) package instant ramen, such as Top Ramen or Maruchan
- 1 large egg
- Toasted sesame seeds, for garnish (optional)

1. Place a medium skillet over medium-high heat. Add the butter. Once melted, add the soy sauce and stir. Add the mushrooms, as well as the white parts of the scallion. Sauté for about 3 minutes, stirring occasionally, until the mushrooms are tender. Stir in the spinach and let wilt for about 30 seconds. Turn off the heat.
2. To a medium saucepot over high heat, add 2 cups water and bring to a boil. Add the ramen noodles and cook for 1 minute, stirring occasionally.
3. Crack the egg into the center of the pot on top of the noodles. Keep the heat at a steady simmer and cook for 2 minutes more, until the whites are fully set. Turn off the heat and stir in the seasoning packet, being careful not to break the egg yolk.
4. Pour the soup into a wide bowl. Lay the mushroom-spinach mixture, including any sauce, onto one side of the bowl. Garnish with the greens of the scallion and the sesame seeds (if using). Eat immediately.

my relationship with joy

I care a lot about joy, even if I'm not driven by providing it for myself. Joy is part of the complete experience. There's a yin to the yang. You know about happiness because of sadness. Joy has to be balanced out with another side. My family is my greatest joy in my life, but because of that, there is tremendous stress and overwhelming worry that lives right there with it. There are small moments when I can help my family in ways that aren't just Band-Aid payments but real, genuine help—whether that is financial, emotional, or spiritual. When I can actually help my family, it washes away my stress in that moment and fills me with so much joy that it cleanses me of all the other emotions and fears, even if just for a moment. That joy is wonderful, but it is quickly replaced with a focus on how to do it again.

But just because I'm not the best at feeling or receiving joy, it doesn't mean I'm not driven by it in other ways to spread it to somebody else. Joy is an energy that can be created and transferred. No matter how bad a day I'm having, it doesn't prevent me from improving the day of a person I run into. I was recently in Scotland making videos and ended up getting food poisoning. I had a pounding migraine. I was miserable. But as I was walking around, I saw a kid, and I could tell he recognized me but was too scared or timid to come up and say hi. I happened to have an extra pair of gloves on me, and I just walked up and gave them to him. He beamed with excitement. We took a picture together, and all of a sudden, both of us were having a better day.

I'm only a little bit famous: I'm famous enough to get invited to fancy award shows, but when I get there, I will still get mistaken for the valet at least once. But I've had the benefit of being around people who are *really famous*, and the great ones have shown me a glimpse of what I can do to spread joy to others.

Some of these stars have been celebrities for twenty-plus years, some longer, some maybe since they were little kids. Some of them are so famous that they *really* can't go outside. They experience every inconvenience I've mentioned in this book, multiplied by a thousand. Some of these people, though, have made a huge impression on me in the way that they have patience for people, in every single moment. They will sign autographs, talk to people, and in many instances find a way to have a real, true human connection, even in the few seconds they have with each person. It may be a performance, but the intention is pure and the joy they give to that person is so true. In some cases, that brief moment will be nothing to the giant celebrity, but it will be something the fan will think about over and over again for decades to come. I'm not saying I will ever achieve, or even want, that kind of fame. But to see people like that handling fame at *that level* inspires me to be the best version of myself, to hopefully have my own twenty-plus years of success doing what I love. I want maintained, sustained success.

You know what has maintained and sustained bringing people joy for multiple generations? Chicken pot pie. It is a hit every single time. This version is made even easier with a double crust made from frozen puff pastry—all cooked up into a simple, beautiful dinner.

→

PREP TIME: **20 MINUTES** COOK TIME: **1 HOUR 20 MINUTES** SERVES **6–8**

DOUBLE-CRUST CHICKEN POT PIE

½ cup salted butter, plus more for greasing
19oz (540g) package frozen puff pastry, thawed overnight in the refrigerator or on the counter for 1 hour
1 tbsp olive oil
1lb (450g) boneless, skinless chicken breast, cut into roughly ½in (1cm) cubes
Kosher or fine sea salt
Freshly ground black pepper
2 cups sliced carrots (about ½in / 1cm thick)
1½ cups sliced celery (about ½in / 1cm thick)
1 cup finely chopped yellow onion
2 garlic cloves, finely chopped
6 tbsp all-purpose flour
1 tsp granulated garlic
2 cups chicken broth
1 cup whole milk
1 tbsp finely chopped fresh thyme leaves, or 1 tsp dried thyme
1 cup frozen peas
1 egg

1. Preheat the oven to 400°F (200°C). Lightly grease a 12-inch (30cm) cast-iron skillet with some butter.
2. Divide the puff pastry into 2 pieces. Roll each piece out to a shape that is as circular as you can get it and is about ¼-inch (5mm) thick, making sure that each piece is at least 12 inches (30cm) wide. Lay one piece of dough in the cast-iron skillet and trim so it fits along the bottom with about ½ inch (1cm) of extra dough pushed up the sides. Reserve the remaining puff pastry piece in the refrigerator. Dock the dough by piercing it several times with a fork. Place the skillet in the oven to parbake for 15 minutes, then remove and set aside to cool. Leave the oven on.
3. Place a Dutch oven or a wide pan over medium-high heat. Add the olive oil and, when it is shimmering, add the chicken and season well with salt and black pepper. Cook the chicken for about 4 minutes, stirring frequently, until just barely cooked through. Remove the chicken and set aside.
4. To the same Dutch oven or wide pan over medium heat, add the butter and let it melt. Add the carrots, celery, onion, and garlic. Season with a pinch of salt and pepper, then cook for about 15 minutes, stirring occasionally, until the carrots are just barely tender but not mushy.
5. Sprinkle the flour and granulated garlic over the top and stir frequently for 1 minute, allowing the flour to toast and distribute. Add the chicken broth, a little at a time, stirring constantly and scraping the bottom of the pot with a wooden spoon to incorporate all the good caramelized bits and ensure nothing burns. Continue adding the broth until it is fully incorporated.
6. Add the milk and thyme and stir. Add the peas and return the chicken to the Dutch oven. Continue cooking, stirring occasionally, until the mixture comes to a simmer, adjusting the heat as needed to maintain a gentle simmer and stirring and scraping the bottom to make sure nothing burns. Simmer for about 7 minutes more, until the texture resembles a hearty stew or gravy.
7. Pour the mixture into the skillet on top of the parbaked puff pastry. Take the remaining puff pastry from the fridge and lay it over the top. Use a knife to cut off and remove any pastry that overhangs the sides of the skillet. Cut four small diagonal slits in the center of the pie to create air vents for steam to escape.
8. In a bowl, make an egg wash by whisking the egg with 1 tablespoon water. Use a brush to paint the top of the puff pastry.
9. Bake for 25 to 30 minutes, until the filling is bubbling and the crust has risen and become golden brown. Allow to cool for a few minutes and then serve. Leftovers can be stored in an airtight container in the refrigerator for up to 5 days.

social media: perception vs. reality (i hate my boss)

Sometimes my life is exactly what people probably expect. In recent months, I have been flying around the world, trying viral restaurant dishes, and filming myself eating the food. Sometimes my life is that simple: I eat food, I react to it, I post the video, and hopefully people watch. A few of those in a day is a nice day, and it sure as heck beats working the grill station at Chipotle, or being forced to fire family men from their construction jobs. But the vast majority of what I actually do every day is pretty different from that. Frequently it is more me staring at a wall, trying to think of something funny to do, or writing pitches to celebrities for collaboration videos, or having phone calls with brands, or planning travel and shoots that are eight months out. Here's the thing: If I have committed to this as a job, then I need to treat it as one. I am my own boss, yeah, but I am a *tough* boss. My job is to figure out how to best please my audience so that they can enjoy the work I'm doing.

That is my obsession. My boss (me) won't ever let me let up until I hang it up for good. I enjoy doing these videos, but it is also *stressful*. If I make two viral videos, I'm happy for maybe an hour, and then it's time to get back out there and make another. I'm not really someone who is capable of giving myself a quota, then clocking out when I hit it. My horrible boss (still me) has me working Monday to Sunday, and if he has an idea, it doesn't matter if it's 2 a.m. or noon—whenever it is, I have to go out there and do it. He doesn't give me a 401K, and there's no health insurance. I make more content and make it as good as I possibly can. There have been multiple times when I have spent a whole day working on a video, moved heaven and earth to make it happen, filmed it over and over, and then sat with it, realized it's not good enough, and then let the whole thing go without ever posting.

People perceive this job as an aspirational career where you can pace yourself and make your own schedule and do whatever you want. People probably think I work forty-five minutes a day. Maybe there are people out there who can do that, but I am certainly not one of them. To do the job the way I do it, my boss (me again) works me in a way that is unsustainable in the long term, and my loved ones are the collateral damage. In this situation, if you do it like me, you are Anne Hathaway *and* Meryl Streep in *The Devil Wears Prada*. You miss weddings and birthday parties. The time management, the prioritization, all of it feels like the Wild West in this moment, with multiple platforms trying to get you to put your content there, and with brands battling to get the right deal with the right creator. I don't know how long this industry will sustain itself, but I feel like I need to capitalize on it in case it all goes away one day.

The truth is, there is money *flying around* right now in the social-media space, and people are competing to get as much of it as they can. I just wish that overwhelming amount of money could go to other jobs and to people who really need it instead: people like teachers and caretakers. When I think about the financial struggles these vastly more important members of the workforce have to go through, it makes me deeply upset. I wish all this money could be distributed to the people who really need it, but this is the backward financial reality we live in right now. I also have to look at it this way: If I don't get this money, somebody else will. As a result, I need to make sure that I'm using that money for good, to help other people, as much as I can.

This is perception versus reality. What people assume is never the full truth. My life is more work than most people expect, but it is also probably more emotionally fulfilling than they expect too. It's like a crepe: People expect them to be sweet. They want them to be vessels for Nutella, whipped cream, strawberries, bananas, and powdered sugar. But a crepe is just a thin pancake. You can make it into whatever you want it to be, even savory. This version is salty, just like my boss (yes, still me). So here is a crepe that defies common American dessert-crepe expectations: a delicious, vegetable-loaded, savory crepe you can make right at home.

PREP TIME: 15 MINUTES COOK TIME: 25 MINUTES SERVES 4-6

BUTTERMILK CREPES WITH SPINACH, MUSHROOMS, AND WHITE CHEDDAR

- 1 cup buttermilk
- 1 cup all-purpose flour
- 2 large eggs
- 2 tbsp salted or unsalted butter, plus more for greasing
- ¼ tsp kosher or fine sea salt, plus more to taste
- ¼ tsp baking soda
- 2 tbsp olive oil
- 1 medium shallot, halved and sliced into thin half moons
- 8oz (225g) cremini mushrooms, sliced
- Freshly ground black pepper, to taste
- 5oz (140g) baby spinach
- 8oz (225g) grated white cheddar

1. Place a 10-inch (25cm) nonstick skillet over medium heat to preheat.
2. Meanwhile, to the jar of a blender, add the buttermilk, flour, eggs, butter, salt, and baking soda. Blend on low speed for about 30 seconds, gradually increasing the speed until the mixture is smooth. Scrape down the sides with a rubber spatula to release any stuck flour and blend again, if necessary. Once the batter is ready, increase the heat under the skillet to medium-high.
3. Lightly grease the skillet with a bit of butter, tilting to spread around the entire pan. Pour in about ¼ cup of the batter, quickly tilting the pan to spread it across the bottom in as even a layer as possible. Cook for about 30 seconds, then use a rubber spatula to lift up an edge. Using the spatula and your fingers, flip the crepe over and cook the other side for about 30 seconds more.
4. Transfer to a plate and repeat with the remaining batter. You should end up with about six crepes. Turn off the heat, but don't clean the pan.
5. Place another wide skillet over medium-high heat. Add the olive oil and, once it is shimmering, add the shallot and a pinch of salt. Cook for about 3 minutes, stirring frequently, until they are browning at the edges.
6. Add the mushrooms and season with salt and freshly ground black pepper. Give them a stir, then add about 1 tablespoon water. Continue cooking for 2 to 3 minutes more, until the mushrooms are tender and the water has almost entirely evaporated.
7. Fold in the spinach and cook for another 60 to 90 seconds, until the greens have wilted down and most of the moisture has evaporated. Season lightly with more salt and black pepper to taste.
8. Place the first skillet back over medium-high heat and grease again with the butter. Grab the plate with crepes and scoop a spoonful of the mushroom mixture on one half of the top crepe, then top with a handful of the cheese (about ⅙ the total amount). Fold in half like a quesadilla, then transfer the crepe to the skillet. Let cook for about 1 minute, until the bottom is lightly browned, then flip and repeat with the other side.
9. Transfer to a plate to serve and repeat with the remaining crepes and filling. Leftovers can be stored in an airtight container in the refrigerator for up to 5 days.

learning to balance

"It's the job," I told them.

"This thing is important, and I need to do it."

"I can't move it."

"I can't change it."

I cancelled on family members constantly. Even when I was there, sometimes I wasn't really there. I would have "important" phone calls come in. They'd ask why I couldn't come to a family reunion, or a birthday party, or a wedding. If I joined, they asked why I couldn't be more present. When I left, they'd ask why I couldn't stay longer. "The job," I'd say. I was blaming everything on the job. But that was never really true, even if I didn't realize it at the time. I thought I didn't *really* have a choice, but the truth is I always did. I chose business opportunities over real life, every single time.

The biggest realization for me was not about needing to work less, funnily enough. It was about learning to be honest with myself and the people around me. I was emotionally off balance all the time because I kept being *surprised* by these so-called work emergencies. But if they kept happening, over and over, and I was the one being surprised... well then, I was the real problem. Emotional stability was a matter of reframing the realities of my work. Instead of missing a family gathering because "work came up," I was instead approaching it with open eyes. Now, in the present, I am finally asking myself: Am I choosing this opportunity over my family, or am I choosing my family over the opportunity? Each option gets weighed appropriately. Instead of reacting haphazardly to the erratic nature of my own life and then apologizing for "work coming up," I anticipate the obvious reality and make informed decisions about what I will do. I don't

> "I didn't apologize for my choices: I thought about them and made them with confidence."

apologize for my choices: I think about them and make them with confidence. This change in attention makes me more stable, more balanced, and a better person to be around. If a great opportunity comes up, I am not just "sorry this came up." Instead, I frame it as I can't believe that something *so exciting* came up that I'm willing to choose it over, say, a birthday party if I have to. Evening out this balance has reduced my anxiety and given me a feeling of full control over my career and my relationships.

Balance and choice are tied together. There is always a choice, even if the options are both bad. I have been so fortunate to say that I have made difficult choices between multiple *great* options. Not everyone has such great fortune, and I try very hard to keep that perspective in mind.

Sometimes, that choice comes down to what you want to have for dinner, and for this recipe, I've got a great one for you. In this instance, you get to choose pleasure, comfort, *and* nutrition all in one beautiful dish.

PREP TIME: **3 MINUTES** COOK TIME: **15 MINUTES** SERVES **4**

I *love* Japanese curry, and there are great brands out there that make delicious little concentrated curry cubes sold in Asian grocery stores or online. All you need to do is choose the fresh vegetables and protein you want, give them a light sauté, let them simmer in some water with a curry block, then serve with white rice. For my version, I'm making a Shrimp and Snow Pea Curry Rice. Shrimp cooks so quickly, and it is complemented perfectly by the tender snap of the bright-green snow peas.

SHRIMP AND SNOW PEA CURRY RICE

1 tbsp salted or unsalted butter
3 garlic cloves, finely chopped
1lb (450g) large shelled raw shrimp, tails removed
Kosher or fine sea salt
1 tsp neutral oil, such as canola or vegetable
1 large or 2 medium shallots, cut into ½in (1cm) half moons
3.9oz (110g) cube Japanese curry paste (see note)
6oz (175g) snow peas, tough stems and tips removed
Steamed white rice, such as short grain or jasmine

1. Set a wide skillet or a Dutch oven over medium-high heat. Add the butter and, once it has melted, add the garlic. Cook for about 2 minutes, stirring occasionally, until just beginning to brown at the edges.
2. Meanwhile, pat the shrimp dry with a paper towel and season lightly with salt. Add the shrimp to the pan in a single layer and cook for about 90 seconds to brown on one side, then flip them over and repeat with the other side, another 90 seconds. Reduce the heat to medium, scoop out the shrimp, and set aside.
3. To the same skillet, add the oil, followed by the shallots and a pinch of salt. Cook for about 1 minute, stirring occasionally, until slightly softened. Add 2½ cups water and increase the heat to high. Once bubbling, reduce the heat and gently simmer, covered, for about 3 minutes more, until the shallots are tender.
4. Add the curry cube and stir until dissolved. Let simmer for 2 minutes, then add the snow peas and shrimp, continue to simmer for 90 seconds, and turn off the heat. Serve in wide bowls alongside the steamed rice.

Note: There are lots of Japanese curry mixes available online and in Japanese markets. Try out different ones and see what you like best. You can also choose the spice level (though I always go with mild). Some curry mixes come in different ounce portions, so just adjust the water amount as needed to get the right consistency.

an unsustainable lifestyle (and the value of imperfection)

Now even though I've talked about balance and choices, I understand this is a wholly unsustainable lifestyle. Being a social-media creator will work for a while, but I know I can't sustain this forever. My obsessive personality is both my greatest strength and my greatest weakness. This obsessiveness is why I'm successful professionally, but also why I'm sometimes very bad at taking care of myself and my own emotional and mental well-being. Total obsessiveness is also the recipe for a life without satisfaction. It is, like social-media creation itself, a growing, hungry monster that will never be full.

This applies to many people in many fields. What do you do after you win the World Series? You can say you're going to Disneyland, but the truth is, you take a little break, and then you try to win another one. I'm not saying I'm comparing myself to these people, but I look at them for inspiration. The world's greatest authors and directors are obsessed with their craft. I have spent multiple years trying to get certain people to make a video with me, whether it's Donald Glover, Willem Dafoe, or Ryan Coogler. When I finally get one of them? It doesn't matter how many millions of views it gets; I'll be happy for a couple of days at most. But then what? It's like nothing ever happened. It's time to find another mountain to climb.

But some fields, like sports and maybe social-media creation too, have a point at which you can't do the work anymore and you need to find something else to focus on. That is what excites me about my own future, whenever this ride comes to an end. The only way I know how to move on from an obsession is to find something else to focus on, something I can fail at and start over with. I always looked

at my obsessive nature as if I were trudging my way toward the end zone with a football tucked under my arm, with eight different people hanging on to my legs, arms, back, and neck. They're trying to pull me to the ground, but I keep taking one small step at a time. No matter how far I get, the goal post just keeps moving back. Maybe eventually, I get pulled to the ground, and I need to find another ball, or another sport, to get dragged through.

But it has to end at some point. Climbing a mountain is fun, but sitting at the top, if the top even exists, sounds boring to me. That's why my life is about the pursuit of perfection, even if I know that perfection is unattainable. In fact, *it being unattainable* is the most appealing part of it. It's like shaping a meatball. You can shape a hundred meatballs, and every single one will be a little bit different. But that is part of the point: You want them to be imperfect. You want them to feel handmade. Nobody wants to eat meatballs made by a robot. It's soulless. It's pointless.

This recipe is for my meatball sub, perfect in its imperfections. Hand-rolled balls, nestled into tomato sauce, served on a roll with Parmesan and mozzarella, but also with some bonus sautéed kale because it's important to eat your vegetables, and this veggie make the meal even more delicious. Now get your hands dirty, and make something human and flawed—it'll taste so much better for it.

Presenting a scholarship to a respected member of the community in LA in 2020, at an event hosted by my favorite baseball player. It was my first time speaking publicly like this.

PREP TIME: 30 MINUTES COOK TIME: 30 MINUTES MAKES 4

MEATBALL SUB WITH SAUTÉED KALE

- ½ cup cubed sourdough bread, crusts removed
- ¼ cup whole milk
- ¼ cup grated yellow or white onion
- ¼ cup grated Parmesan cheese, plus more for topping
- 8 garlic cloves, finely chopped, divided
- 2 tbsp finely chopped parsley
- 3 tbsp olive oil, divided, plus more for hands
- 1 egg
- 1 tsp dried oregano
- ½ tbsp kosher or fine sea salt, plus more to taste
- Freshly ground black pepper
- 1lb (450g) 80% lean ground beef
- 1 bunch (8–12 leaves) of Tuscan kale, stems removed, leaves sliced into 1in (2.5cm) strips
- 28oz (794g) can whole, peeled tomatoes, crushed by hand
- 1 sprig of basil, or 1 tbsp dried basil, chopped
- Four 6in (15cm) hoagie rolls, split open
- 8 sandwich-style slices of low-moisture mozzarella

Note: You can make fewer sandwiches, and leftover kale and meatballs can be stored in the refrigerator for up to 1 week and reheated in a covered pot with tomato sauce.

1. To a medium mixing bowl, add the bread cubes and milk and let soak for about 5 minutes, stirring occasionally, until the milk is fully absorbed. Meanwhile, in a large mixing bowl, combine the onion, Parmesan, three of the garlic cloves, the parsley, 1 tablespoon of the olive oil, the egg, and dried oregano.
2. Once the bread is soaked, crumble it with your fingers and add it to the large mixing bowl. Season with the salt and several twists of freshly ground black pepper. Stir the mixture until well combined, then add the ground beef and fold together until very well mixed.
3. Lightly oil your hands, then form the mixture into golf ball–size meatballs (you should get around sixteen), and set them aside on a plate.
4. Place a 12-inch (30cm) cast-iron skillet over medium-high heat and allow it to preheat for about 3 minutes. Once hot, add the remaining 2 tablespoons olive oil and then arrange the meatballs in a single layer in the pan. These are tender meatballs, so be careful not to knock them around too much. Cook for 2 to 3 minutes, until they have a nice golden-brown sear on the bottom. Using tongs, carefully flip each one and sear the other side for another 2 to 3 minutes. You want a nice bit of browning on both sides, but don't worry about cooking them all the way through, as they will finish in the sauce. Once they are seared, carefully transfer them to a plate and reduce the heat to low.
5. To the pan, add two of the remaining garlic cloves and let them sizzle for about 30 seconds, then add the kale and a pinch of salt. Set the heat to medium and cook for about 3 minutes, stirring occasionally, until the kale is just tender. Use tongs to remove the kale and set aside in a bowl or plate.
6. Add the remaining three garlic cloves to the pan and cook for about 3 minutes, until just brown at the edges. Add the tomatoes, a pinch of salt, a few twists of freshly ground black pepper, and the basil. Increase the heat to medium-high and bring to a simmer. Reduce the heat to a gentle simmer and cook for about 5 minutes, then taste and season with salt as needed.
7. Return the meatballs to the pan. Allow them to simmer in the sauce for about 2 minutes, just to finish cooking them, gently shaking the pan from time to time. Turn off the heat.
8. Quickly toast the hoagie rolls in a toaster oven (unless they are very fresh) or wrap them in a paper towel and microwave them for 15 seconds. Open the hoagies and lay one piece of mozzarella on the bottom slice of each roll. Spoon four meatballs, along with some sauce, into each sandwich. Add ¼ of the kale to each sandwich, next to the meatballs.
9. Top with the grated Parmesan and close the sandwiches. Serve as is or wrapped in parchment paper and sliced in half, with more warm sauce on the side.

NIKE

is social media bad?

There are two sides to social media: creating content and watching content.

From a creator standpoint, I get very scared about how much of a desired career path it has become for a lot of kids. If I polled a classroom of thirty middle-school kids when I was growing up, maybe two or three of them would have wanted to be musicians or actors or athletes. Now, based on my days substitute teaching and the comments I see online, it feels like most kids want to be social-media stars or streamers. They think it's the coolest thing in the world. While I will happily admit that social media has some incredibly positive sides that can improve people's lives and communities, we have to be so careful about the intention behind the things we create.

Right now, in the year 2026, it feels like so many people view social-media stardom as the only attainable path to financial survival and growth—an opportunity for a leg up and a chance to get some breathing room in a difficult world and in a difficult economy. What saddens me so much is not that social media is an avenue for this, but that it might be the only one for a lot of folks. The financial possibilities make a career in social media incredibly enticing, but it becomes a force for desperation when there aren't as many attainable jobs in which people can invest their time, make a real living, and support their families. This economic reality makes for a sad state of affairs, and it also creates a very difficult environment for content creation itself. Vast monetary opportunities can lure people who are doing it just for financial success or perks rather than for the love of creation itself. I think social media is better for the creators and the audience when there is a love of the game that is tied through all of it.

My first picture taken with my mangers, Michael Berkowitz and Doug Landers, when we met at an event in 2021. I actually had confidence my life was gonna be changing for the better, and I'd be able to provide for my family.

When creativity doesn't come from a desire to share your voice and develop your art, it ends up being only about growth and success. Some of those people, mind you, become very successful. The people in some of these fields claim to earn tens of millions of dollars per year. But in my opinion, when you create for exclusively financial reasons, you will burn out. You will change as a person, and it will be a long time before you realize that you don't love the person you've become—if you ever even notice it. I would never tell my loved ones to become social-media content creators. If they love it, I hope they do it from a place of joy and of excitement to create. But if it's your goal to make this a full-time career just as a way of making money while looking at it as a burden rather than a blessing? That's a path to a darker world for you and your audience.

It is important, I think, as audience members (and remember that we creators are audience members too) to be more selective in what we give our attention to. Endless scrolling can lead to discovery, but it can also lead to listless wandering, keeping you watching the next video and the next in an infinite loop. Social media, like anything in life, needs to be balanced out. Don't just watch social media. I hope you watch *The Godfather*, as well, even though it can seem incredibly slow by comparison (and don't tell me you've "seen most of it in TikTok clips"). Read books. Read a newspaper, even if the information is all incredibly old by the time you get it in your hands. Sit through dialogue and exposition. Go back and find old movies, and not just the sequels and remakes they try to throw at us. Allow your mind to accept all these different worlds of storytelling. The human brain is delicate, but it is also capable of being reshaped. None of these things are inherently bad, but too much of anything is unhealthy. Heck, even if you ate only broccoli for the rest of your life, you would be lacking in a lot of important nutrients. Life requires balance, in all instances.

Is social media bad? No, not on its own. But it can be used for evil. It's up to us, and the future creators and audience members, to help mold it in the right direction.

If you are a social-media creator out there, or an aspiring one who is reading this book, hoping to find out the secret, here's the best one I can offer: Create content online because you love it. Enjoy it,

> "Social media, like anything in life, needs to be balanced out."

be creative, and try to shoot your shot and make something you're proud of. Chase creativity, not likes. Think about the best basketball players in the world. If there was no NBA and no way to make money from basketball, they would still be out there on the court, giving it everything they have. That's what you should be aspiring toward. Make that money if it is there, yes, but always put the game, or that sense of creative passion, ahead of the business.

Find something you are excited about and make it. This leads me to the next recipe, Red Velvet Cheesecake Brownies, made famous by Broma Bakery, an incredibly popular baking blog based in Brooklyn, NY. I first experienced this back in 2024 and loved it so much that I made an at-home version, inspired by Sarah Fennel's dish, amping up a box of brownie mix and taking it to the next level with her signature swirl.

PREP TIME: 10 MINUTES COOK TIME: 40 MINUTES MAKES 16

RED VELVET CHEESECAKE BROWNIES

- Nonstick spray
- 16.3oz (462g) box chocolate brownie mix, such as Betty Crocker Favorites Milk Chocolate Brownie
- ½ cup vegetable oil
- 3 eggs, at room temperature, divided
- 2 tsp red food coloring
- 6oz (175g) cream cheese, at room temperature
- ⅓ cup granulated white sugar

1. Preheat the oven to 350°F (180°C). Line a 9 x 9-inch (23 x 23cm) baking dish or brownie pan with parchment paper and spray with nonstick spray.
2. In a medium mixing bowl, add the brownie mix, vegetable oil, 2 tablespoons water, two of the eggs, and the food coloring. Whisk until well combined, then spread the batter into the prepared baking dish in an even layer.
3. To another medium mixing bowl, add the cream cheese, the remaining egg, and the sugar and whisk until smooth.
4. Dollop the cream-cheese mixture onto the top of the brownie mixture in big plops, then use a butter knife to drag big, decorative swirls throughout the batter.
5. Bake for 35 to 40 minutes, until a toothpick or knife inserted into the middle comes out clean. Allow to cool, then slice into 16 small brownies, and enjoy. Leftovers can be stored in an airtight container in the refrigerator for up to 1 week.

what is success?

Success can mean a lot of different things to different people. Many might see my millions of followers and deem me successful. That is a kind of success, to be sure. But when I look back at my life, that will not be how I judge myself. I have become a person who has learned to compete against myself. If you compete against yourself, you can always improve. But competing against yourself also means you can never win. There will always be another level to attain. To me, success will be achieved when I have learned not to be fueled by obsession.

But there's also this: I have a checklist of things that I have always wanted to achieve with my videos. It is a list of people I want to work with, along with some goals I want to reach. But to reach my goals, I actually don't need to complete each task. I just need to know that I have worked as hard as I possibly could, and if I do that, I am able to live with the results. I don't want to look at anything in my life that I cared about and say I failed because I didn't work hard enough. To be perfectly honest, that list is getting closer and closer to being completed. So, when that happens, what's next?

For this part of my life, success is about being able to provide for my family—to put a roof over their head that can never go away. Success is about being able to help others. I'm closer to the end of this chapter of my life than I am to the beginning. I want to use what I've gained to hold the door open for other people. I want to seek out those who are building content for the right reasons and help them to amplify their voices. This can quickly become a "who do you know?" business, and I want to be the one who can aid in letting deserving people break through, who maybe didn't have the access they needed. To help others would be a way of satiating and appeasing

that obsession in my soul. I want to pour that energy back into my community, to the people who are hungry to tell their stories, to heal the landscape that surrounds all of us.

So where do I see my future in social media? I see it as a thing I am getting closer and closer to stepping back from—in order to move forward. Every great thing that we love ends at some point. I have gotten to control my story, and it is one of the best feelings in the world. I want to be a part of the ending of this chapter too. It is an amazing thing to have power over the beginning and the end of this part of my life, and the telling of that story.

I want to end it on my terms. I want to end it in Utah like Michael Jordan, holding up my follow-through and winning my sixth title with the Chicago Bulls. I want to end it in a Bulls jersey, so to speak, instead of a Wizards jersey. The way to do that is to find new things to be passionate about, and to find the next journey. I'm not stepping back just yet, but know that when I do, it will be for all the right reasons, and with a new chapter, with more things to create . . . just at a different pace, and in a different way.

This last recipe in my book will end in the way so much of my food story began: with fast food. It ends with one of the most perfect creations: the Taco Bell Crunchwrap Supreme. Is a recipe for a homemade Crunchwrap a silly way to end a book? Maybe. Or maybe it's a reminder for all of us that sometimes you don't need to take life too seriously and to be okay with giving yourself exactly what you want.

PREP TIME: **10 MINUTES** COOK TIME: **1 HOUR** MAKES **12**

CRUNCHWRAP SUPREME

2 tbsp corn oil or neutral oil, such as canola or vegetable
1lb (450g) ground beef
Kosher or fine sea salt, to taste
1½ tsp cayenne pepper
1 tsp smoked paprika
½ tsp granulated white sugar
½ tsp cumin
½ tsp granulated garlic
½ tsp granulated onion
Twelve 12in (30cm) flour tortillas
15oz (425g) can nacho cheese
Twelve 6in (15cm) tostada shells
¾ cup sour cream
½ head of iceberg lettuce, shredded
3 large tomatoes, diced (optional)

1. Place a wide skillet over medium-high heat. Add the oil and, once it is shimmering, add the ground beef and a pinch of salt. Cook for about 5 minutes, stirring frequently and breaking up the beef with a wooden spoon, until most of the raw color is cooked out.
2. Add the cayenne, paprika, sugar, cumin, granulated garlic, granulated onion, and 2 teaspoons water. Stir to combine and continue cooking for about 1 more minute, until most of the liquid evaporates. It should be ever so slightly saucy. If the mixture is too dry, add a touch more water. If it's too wet, continue cooking to evaporate. Remove from the heat and set aside. Taste for seasoning and add salt as needed.
3. Place a nonstick or cast-iron skillet or griddle over medium to medium-high heat. Place one tortilla in the pan and heat for about 30 seconds per side, until pliable enough to shape without breaking. Keep the pan hot.
4. On a clean work surface, lay the tortilla down, then put a generous spoonful of the beef in the center, spreading it in a single layer to about the width of a tostada shell. Dollop about 2 tablespoons of the nacho cheese over the beef, then lay the tostada on top. Spread 2 tablespoons of the sour cream on the tostada, then sprinkle with a layer of shredded iceberg. Top with about 2 tablespoons of the diced tomatoes (if using; if you're me, you don't!).
5. Next, you are going make six slightly overlapping folds to form a tightly sealed hexagon. The trick is to evenly space out the folds, pressing as you go to keep a tight seal. Take one edge of the tortilla and fold it toward the center of the filling. Hold it in place with one hand, then take the next section of the tortilla and fold toward the center, overlapping slightly with the previous fold. Repeat this process, making four more folds and trying your best to hold tightly in place.
6. Carefully lay the wrap fold-side down back in the hot pan, pressing down slightly with a spatula to create as much contact with the pan as possible. Adjust the heat as needed, slowly searing for 1½ to 2 minutes, until the bottom is a deep golden-brown and not burned. Flip and repeat, browning the other side.
7. Enjoy while hot, repeating to make as many as you want to eat. Leftover filling can be stored, covered, in the refrigerator for up to 1 week.

ACKNOWLEDGMENTS

I'd like to thank my mom, dad, and brother for their support throughout my journey.

Clockwise from top left: When I started training to walk on to UC Riverside in 2018; with my mom and my brother—we went to a play at the theater where I used to work when I was sixteen; with my best friend Jonah at my first ever Dodgers game.

INDEX by MEAL TYPE

INDEX

D

E

F

G

H

I

J

K